The Intelligent Heart, The Pure Heart

The
Intelligent Heart,
The Pure Heart

An insight into the Heart based on
the Qur'an, Sunnah and Modern Science

DR. GOHAR MUSHTAQ

Ta-Ha Publishers Ltd.

Copyright © **Ta-Ha Publishers Ltd.** 1427AH/2006

First published March 2006
Second Edition printed May 2008

Published by
Ta-Ha Publishers Ltd.
Unit 4, The Windsor Centre
Windsor Grove, London, SE27 9NT
www.taha.co.uk

Written by Dr. Gohar Mushtaq
Edited by Dr. Abia Afsar-Siddiqui

British Library Cataloguing in Publication Data
Mushtaq, Gohar, 1971
The intelligent heart, the pure heart: an insight into the heart based on the Qur'an
Sunnah and modern science
1. Heart – Religious aspects – Islam
I. Title II. Afsar-Siddiqui, Abia
297.5
ISBN-10: 1-84200-075-6
ISBN-13: 978-1-84200-075-5

Printed and bound in the UK by De-Luxe Printers Ltd., London

Cover/Book design and typeset by Shakir Cadir at Open Squares Ltd.
www.opensquares.co.uk

Table of Contents

The Heart and *Tawaf* (Circumambulation of the Ka'bah)
The Heart and the Acceptance of Islam
The Heart and the Mother-Child Bond

Acknowledgements

I WOULD LIKE to express my special thanks to Sheikh Hamza Yusuf (director of the Zaytuna Institute, California), Paul Pearsall, Ph.D. (author of 'The Heart's Code') and Doc Childre & Rollin McCraty of the HeartMath Institute because their research on the human heart has been very valuable for me. I would also like to thank Dr. Abia Afsar-Siddiqui of Ta-Ha Publishers Ltd. for her patience in editing the manuscript of my book and her deep and insightful comments about it. I owe a debt of gratitude to my parents, Mushtaq Choudhry and Farida Mushtaq, for not only teaching me about Islamic Sciences but also for their encouragement to me in this project. My mother-in-law (and my aunt) Khalida Ishtiaq also deserves many thanks. As with my previous book, again I am deeply thankful to my wife, Sadia Gohar, because this research would have been extremely hard without her relentless support for me.

Foreword

THE INTELLIGENT HEART, The Pure Heart by Dr. Gohar Mushtaq is a bold effort to render concept to the ubiquitous adage in almost all literary writings and in common verbal usage of the heart as an organ of intellect with the capacity for rational thought, inference and discrimination. Affection, emotion, love, hate, courage and a multitude of other words are used in relation to the heart to depict it as having the capacity of intellect, judgement and capable of distinguishing good from evil.

Old scriptures and religious books including The Holy Qur'an frequently refer to the heart as an organ of understanding and judgement. Gohar Mushtaq has given numerous references and quotes to this effect. This is the impetus for his writing the book; he has presented scientific facts and evidence substantiating the role of the heart. I found myself eager to keep reading to find the evidence provided. I am sure the reader will as well.

This book is not an attempt to compare the functioning of the brain with that of the heart, as pointed out by the author in the text, "The purpose of the research in this book is not to negate the importance of the brain but to emphasise the importance of the heart"; it may seem like that in some passages, though, to the questioning reader. Finally the reader will find himself clearly agreeing that the brain is the repository of knowledge, of learning, ascertaining, satisfying curiosity, memory and all aspects of embedding, storage and quick retrieval and calculations. The reader will also find, given the abundance of facts and quotes, substantiated to an extent scientifically in conjunction with sufficient present understanding of literary writings and experiences, that the heart does possess an ability to affect the brain and play a role in understanding and intellect.

This book contains compelling examples to initiate a process of thinking for the curious and investigative mind. Somehow we will all agree that if the heart is not inclined we rarely feel good. This feeling from the heart is after all the driving message of the book; the distinction between good and bad, the cure for the heart after all is the contented heart!

I will end with a hadith quoted in this book and a verse from The Holy Qur'an.

> On the authority of Wabisa bin Mabad ﷺ who came to the Messenger of Allah ﷺ: "You have come to ask about righteousness?" I said: "Yes." He said: "Consult your heart. Righteousness is that about which the soul feels tranquil and the heart feels tranquil, and wrongdoing is that which wavers in the soul and moves back and forth in the breast even though people again and again have given you their opinion in its favour." *(Ahmad and Ad-Darimi)*

And surely, We have created many of the jinns and mankind for Hell. They have hearts wherewith they understand not, they have eyes wherewith they see not, and they have ears wherewith they hear not (the Truth). (Surah Al-A'raf: 179)

Ali A. Javed, Ph.D. (Genetics)
New York, 2004

Preface

TODAY WE ARE living in an age of materialism; an age of anti-spiritualism, or the age most suitable for the coming of the anti-Christ. Modern science is a result of the revolt of scientists and the masses against the Church in the West. At the very foundation of modern scientific thought lie the materialist philosophies of Comte, Hegel, Durkheim, Nietzsche, Freud, Marx and Darwin. As a consequence of that, the spiritual aspect of the human personality is deliberately ignored in modern science. Hence, we see the body/soul split in this age of materialism. It is because of the body/soul split we find in modern biomedicine and the social sciences that most of the research has been conducted on the human brain whereas the human heart has been regarded as merely a pumping organ. Today, the separation of the heart and brain is a consequence of the separation of religious and secular matters in the Western educational system and society in general.

Nevertheless, in the last twenty years, some interesting research has been conducted on the human heart in the fields of biomedicine, psychology and social science, showing that the heart possesses its own kind of intelligence and it affects the brain in various ways.

This research is still in its incipient stages. It will take some time for the secular mainstream scientific community to accept these research findings. It is evident from the history of science that many scientific discoveries faced opposition in the beginning but later they were accepted as universal facts. A few decades ago, Rudolf Steiner, a German philosopher and education expert, noted that:

> "The greatest discovery of twentieth century science would be that the heart is not a pump but vastly more, and that the great challenge of the coming ages of humanity would be, in effect, to allow the heart to teach us to think in a new way." [1]

It seems that now the time has come for us to realise that the human heart is not just a pumping organ but much more than that. The days of Newtonian mechanics, in which the human heart was regarded as a mere pumping organ, will soon become a concept of the past.

It may be of interest to readers to mention the reason that acted as an impetus in my writing this book. The subject of the intelligence of the human heart as it is mentioned in religious scriptures has always fascinated me. During my high school years in the 1980's, I was once watching a lecture about the function of the human heart by a surgeon on television. During the course of his lecture, the surgeon mentioned that there is no intelligence or emotion in the human heart. At that time I did not have any scientific proof

---

1. Pearce, Joseph Chilton (1998), *Waking Up to the Holographic Heart: Starting over with Education.* Wild Duck Review IV (2)

to refute his claim. However, that incident further triggered my interest in this subject and I started to research the subject of the intelligence of the human heart.

Qur'anic statements are all true and it is only time and knowledge that precludes our immediate understanding of them. It will take modern science many years to fully understand the wisdom behind the verses (*ayat*) of the Qur'an. The human heart is regarded as an organ of intellect in various places throughout the Qur'an. Sooner or later, modern science will also reach this conclusion. It was this miraculous aspect (*ijaaz*) of the Qur'an, which was mentioned by Abdullah bin Abbas (the great commentator of the Qur'an and cousin of the Prophet ﷺ) when he said:

> (In this book of Allah) there are signs (*ayat*), which will only be explained with the passing of time.

Another factor which incited me and excited me to write this book is the fact that recently my book entitled *Growing a Beard: In Light of the Qur'an, Sunnah and Modern Science* [2] has been published. In that book, I had accentuated the importance of an outward aspect (*zahir*) of Islam. I felt a need to also emphasise the inward aspect (*batin*) of Islam by writing on the subject of the human heart since Islam is a balance between the outward and the inward (*zahir and batin*). We need to purify ourselves both inwardly and outwardly to reach the final stage of '*nafs ul-mutma'innah*' (the peaceful self), a state of inner peace and contentment.

---

2. Mushtaq, Gohar (2003), *Growing a Beard: In Light of the Qur'an, Sunnah and Modern Science*. London, Ta-Ha Publishers.

The first part of this book puts into context the human heart according to the Qur'an and hadith (the traditions of the Prophet Muhammad ﷺ), comments of Islamic theologians and contemporary scientific research. The second chapter of this book delves deeper into the concept of intelligence of the heart and the relationship between the heart and the brain. The third chapter highlights the role of the heart within Islam and how our everyday lives as Muslims affect the heart, something which is becoming clearer only now with the passage of time. The fourth and final chapter of this book, which I think can be considered as the most important, discusses the various diseases of the heart, physical and spiritual, and outlines their cures according to the Qur'an and Sunnah.

I have made every attempt to make the scientific language in the book as simple as possible for non-science readers. I would like to mention this point very clearly right at the beginning of this book that the purpose of presenting scientific research regarding the heart as an organ of intelligence is not to prove that the Qur'an is the word of Allah because we already know as part of our faith that Qur'an is indeed the word of Allah. The purpose of presenting this research is to discover some of the details of the Qur'anic and Prophetic wisdoms as they have become available through modern scientific research, so that these research findings can be presented as such in this context to both Muslims and non-Muslims. The Qur'an encourages us to reflect upon the creations of Allah at various places and emphasises the importance of knowledge by telling us:

Say: 'Are those who know equal to those who know not?'
(Surah Az-Zumar: 9)

It is only those who have knowledge among His slaves that fear Allah.
(Surah Fatir: 28)

Gohar Mushtaq
Ph.D. (Biophysical & Biochemistry)
Connecticut, U.S.A.
October 2005

CHAPTER ONE

The Heart is More than Just a Pump...

FOR CENTURIES, religious scriptures, poets, physicians and philosophers have regarded the heart as the centre of our personality, the core of our being. In every language and tradition throughout the world, there are numerous phrases expressed in terms of the heart. A lover may 'steal your heart'; an unfeeling person is 'hard-hearted'; a generous person is 'warm-hearted'; while someone who works with full devotion is said to be working 'whole-heartedly'. When people are asked to point to themselves, they usually point to the region of their bodies where the heart resides. This chapter is a brief introduction to this important organ in the light of the Qur'an, Hadith, Muslim theologians and modern science.

The Heart according to the Qur'an and the Hadith

The Arabic word for heart is *qalb* (from the verb *qalaba* meaning 'to turn about or upside down') and it appears some 130 times in the Qur'an. It is referred to as the seat of affection and emotion, a quality that we all readily associate with the heart:

And He has united their (i.e. believers') hearts. (Surah Al-Anfal: 63)

However, the Qur'an also clearly specifies the human heart as the centre of intellect[3] and wisdom:

...They have hearts wherewith they understand not... (Surah Al-A'raf: 179)

Have they not travelled through the land, and have they hearts wherewith to understand and ears wherewith to hear? Verily, it is not the eyes that grow blind, but it is the hearts which are in the breasts that grow blind. (Surah Al-Hajj: 46)

Verily, therein is indeed a reminder for him who has a heart or gives ear while he is heedful. (Surah Qaf: 37)

These *ayat* reveal that the heart is a sensory organ that possesses the faculties of insight and understanding and, if perceptive, is capable of recognising truth. Such a heart is described in the Qur'an as being satisfied (13:28), wide awake (50:37) and strong (18:14). Conversely, the heart that refuses to recognise the Divine Truth is described in the Qur'an as hard (6:43), sealed (9:87), tainted (2:283) and diseased (8:49).

While it is true that when the Qur'an speaks of *al-qalb*, it encompasses more than the physical heart, it is important to remember that it is within the physical heart that the spiritual heart resides. Therefore, the physical heart can be regarded as the

---

3. The word intellect derives from the Latin 'intellectus' which means the faculty that can perceive the transcendent – a quality of the heart.

point of interaction between the human body and the spiritual *qalb*.[4] The physical heart acts like a gateway to the human soul. The implication of this is that the physical heart is not just a pumping organ, but that it must have the qualities of intelligence that are mentioned in the Qur'an.

The word *fu'ad* has been used in the Qur'an to describe the faculties of the heart. It literally means 'a place of benefit' but carries the meaning of both feeling and rational thinking and is often mentioned in conjunction with the faculties of hearing (*sama'*) and seeing (*basar*):

> *And Allah has brought you out from the wombs of your mothers while you know nothing. And He gave you hearing, sight and hearts that you might give thanks (to Allah).* (Surah An-Nahl: 78)

> *And follow not that of which you have no knowledge. Verily, the hearing, and the sight, and the heart, of each of those you will be questioned (by Allah).* (Surah Al-Isra: 36)

In these *ayat*, the words *sama'*, *basar* and *fu'ad* are used for the three faculties of hearing, seeing and thinking/feeling, which are associated with the ears, eyes and the heart respectively. These are not as unrelated as they first appear to be. The ears and eyes provide information from one's environment, but it is the heart that compiles, analyses and interprets the raw information that has been supplied to it through the ears and eyes. The processed information then governs our actions. The faculty of hearing is

---

4. Haq, Manzurul, *'Heart': The Locus of Human Psyche* in Ansari, Z. A., Ed. (1981). *Qur'anic Concepts of Human Psyche*. Islamabad, International Institute of Islamic Thought.

mentioned before sight because at birth the sense of hearing is fully functional whereas it takes some weeks for the sense of sight to fully develop so that a baby can recognise distant objects and faces. The heart is mentioned last of all because the faculty of understanding takes many years to develop.

The importance of the heart is re-iterated in the Hadith as an-Nu'man bin Bashir reported that the Prophet Muhammad ﷺ said:

> ...Indeed there is in the body a piece of flesh which if it is sound then the whole body is sound, and if it is corrupt then the whole body is corrupt. Indeed it is the heart.
> *(Bukhari and Muslim)*

In the commentary of this tradition, Ibn Rajab Hanbali stated that we can regard the heart as the ruler of all the organs of the body and all the organs are its obedient soldiers. If the king is pious, all the soldiers will remain pious and if the king becomes corrupt, all the soldiers will also become corrupt.[5] The corruption of the body by the defective heart refers to both physical diseases as well as spiritual diseases as will be shown later in this book.

Another hadith reported by Wabisa bin Mabad ﷺ elucidates the role of the heart:

> I went to the Messenger of Allah ﷺ and he asked me, "Have you come to enquire about piety?" I replied in the affirmative.

---

5. Ibn Rajab, Hanbali (1995). *Jami al-Uloom wal Hukam (Commentary on An-Nawawi's Forty Ahadith)* (Urdu language). Lahore, Al-Faisal Publishers & Booksellers

Then he said, "Ask your heart regarding it. Piety is that which contents the soul and comforts the heart, and sin is that which causes doubts and perturbs the heart, even if people pronounce it lawful and give you verdicts on such matters again and again." *(Ahmad and Ad-Darimi)*

This hadith reveals that the heart is the organ that leads one to piety. The pious man has a contented heart, is firm in his action and collected in mind. The sinful man, however, has doubt in his heart, which takes away all stability of action and causes the self to be restless as the Qur'an states:

…And whose hearts are in doubt that ask your leave. So in their doubts they waver. (Surah At-Tawbah: 45)

The Heart according to Muslim Theologians

The role of the heart in the human body has been acknowledged and well understood for centuries by Islamic theologians and mystics.

Imam Ghazali, in his intellectual masterpiece, *Ihya Ulum ad-Din* (Revival of the Islamic Sciences), wrote in detail about the human heart:

"Although the spiritual heart (*qalb*), which is the controlling centre of the soul, is different from the physical human heart, its functioning is related and directed by it…. Every quality that appears in the heart will have its influence flowing to the organs so they act only in accordance with that quality. In the same manner, the effect of every action that is committed from the organs may reach the heart. And this keeps on occurring in a circular fashion." [6]

Abdur Rahman Ibn al-Jawzee, in his book, *Minhajul Qasideen,* expressed the following views about the human heart:

"We should understand that the heart holds the supreme position in the human body. It is this organ that recognises Allah and works to get close to Allah. Other organs are its subordinates. The heart by its nature quests for the path of righteousness. It is true that whoever has recognised his heart has recognised Allah." [7]

Ibn al-Qayyim al-Jawziya, while discussing the relationship between the human heart and mind stated:

"The truth, however, seems to be that the intellectual function starts at the heart, then finds its elaboration and fruitation in the head." [8]

Maulana Jalaluddin Rumi, the Islamic theologian and poet, mentioned the intelligence of the human heart in his famous *Mathnawi* in the following poetic verses:

---

6. Ghazali, Imam Abu Hamid (1978). *Ihya Ulum ad-Din.* Karachi, Darul Isha'at Publishers.
7. Ibn al-Jawzee, Imam Abdur Rahman (1992). *Minhajul Qasideen.* Lahore, Idara Marif Islami Publishers.
8. Al-Qoz, Anas Abdul-Hameed (Capt.) (2000). *Men & The Universe: Reflections of Ibn Al-Qayyim.* Riyadh, Darussalam.

"There are two kinds of intelligence.
One is like that acquired by a child at school,
From books and teachers, new ideas and memorisation.
Your intelligence may become superior to others,
But retaining all that knowledge is a heavy load.
You who are occupied in searching for knowledge
are a preserving tablet,
But the preserved tablet is the one who has gone beyond all this.
For the other kind of intelligence is the gift of God:
Its fountain is in the midst of the soul.
When the water of God-given knowledge gushes from the breast,
It doesn't become fetid or impure.
And if its way to the outside is blocked, what harm is there?
For it gushes continually from the house of the heart.
The acquired intelligence is like the conduits
which run into the house from the streets:
If those pipes become blocked, the house is bereft of water.
Seek the fountain from within yourself." [9]
(Mathnawi Vol. IV, 1960-68)

It is worthwhile noting that these scholars wrote about the function of the human heart and its faculty of intellect with such clarity at a time when no sophisticated biomedical engineering instruments were available, yet their insights into the workings of the heart appear to be those of a modern scientist.

---

9. Helminski, Kabir (1999), *The Knowing Heart: A Sufi Path of Transformation*. Boston, Shambhala Publications.

The Heart according to Modern Science

The analogy of the heart to a pump was first made in the nineteenth century. The steam engine had just been invented and the pumping movements of its pistons impressed physiologists to the extent that they likened this motion to that of the heart.[10]

Even if we look at the pumping efficiency alone of the heart, it is remarkable. The heart beats about 100,000 times a day, forty million times a year and it beats non-stop throughout a lifetime. It pumps two gallons of blood per minute and over 100 gallons per hour. The vascular system that is transporting this life-giving blood around the body is over 60,000 miles long, which is more than twice the circumference of the earth.[11] From the moment it begins beating (around week twelve of gestation) until the moment it stops, the human heart works tirelessly. In an average lifetime, the heart beats more than two and a half billion times without ever pausing to rest.

However, science has now conceded that which the Qur'an stated fourteen centuries ago – that the heart is not just a pumping organ. Recently, a new medical field known as neurocardiology has emerged, which studies the science of the nervous system in the heart. J. Andrew Armour, M.D., Ph.D., is a pioneer in the field of neurocardiology for his groundbreaking research in the area of anatomy and function of the heart's intrinsic nervous system. He has uncovered the presence of neurons in the heart; the same type

10. Pearce, Joseph Chilton (2002). *The Biology of Transcendence*. Rochester, Vermont, Park Street Press.
11. Schiefelbein, S. The Powerful River. In: Poole, R. ed. (1986). *The Incredible Machine*. Washington, D.C., The National Geographic Society.

of cells that are also present in the human brain. There are over 40,000 of these neurons in a human heart – a quantity comparable to a small centre of the human brain. Furthermore, the nervous system of the heart is made up of these neurons, which are capable of processing information without the help of neurons from the brain. The neurons of the heart obtain information from the rest of the body and make appropriate adjustments and send back this information from the heart to the rest of the body including the brain. In addition to this, these neurons possess a kind of short-term memory, which allows them to function independently of the central nervous system. These findings prompted Armour to refer to the nervous system of the heart as the "little brain in the heart"[12] and he draws the following conclusions about the functions of the heart as a result of his research:

"The heart possesses its own little brain, capable of complex computational analysis on its own. Data clearly indicate that the intrinsic cardiac nervous system acts as much more than a simple relay station for the extrinsic autonomic projections to the heart…

An understanding of the complex anatomy and function of the heart's nervous system contributes an additional dimension to the newly emerging view of the heart as a sophisticated information processing centre, functioning not only in concert with the brain but also independent of it."[13]

---

12. Armour, J. Andrew, M.D., Ph.D. & Ardell, Jeffry L., Ph.D. ed. (1994). *Neurocardiology*. New York, Oxford University Press.
13. Armour, J. Andrew, M.D., Ph.D. (2003). *Neurocardiology: Anatomical and Functional Principles*. Boulder Creek, California, Institute of HeartMath.

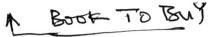

(7) SEVEN KINDS OF INTELLIGENCE

① Linguistic →   The two I Q
                 measures

② Musical

③ Logical Mathematical

④ Spatial (position, area, and si
           of thing in relation to

⑤ Bodily-Kinesthetic

⑥ Intrapersonal (dealing with ow
                     (own knowledge

⑦ Interpersonal (dealing with
                     (knowledge of othe

Dr Howard Gardner :- Harvard Unive

Book :- FRAMES of MIND

PS :- He revolutionised the whole conc
      of intelligence

CHAPTER TWO

The Intelligence of the Heart

THERE IS NO doubt that both the human brain and the human heart possess intelligence. However, the intelligence of the heart and that of the brain are not the same and as a consequence the two organs perceive truth and reality in different ways. This chapter discusses the differences in the two organs and their relationship with each other.

What is Intelligence?

Prior to the 1980's, it was widely believed that there was only one kind of intelligence, expressed by the brain and measurable through IQ (Intelligence Quotient) tests. In 1983, Howard Gardner, the Harvard University researcher and developmental psychologist, in his book 'Frames of Mind', revolutionised the whole concept of intelligence. He propounded that there are different kinds of intelligence such as linguistic, musical, logical-mathematical, spatial, bodily-kinesthetic, intrapersonal (dealing with one's own knowledge) and interpersonal (dealing with knowledge of others).[14] Gardner's theory of multiple types of intelligence is in stark contrast with the prevailing scientific view of intelligence as a single, general faculty of the mind. According to Dr. Gardner, every person possesses a blend of these seven kinds of intelligence, most of which are overlooked in our educational system. Hence, intelligence is far more complex than an IQ rating would suggest. An IQ test only measures two aspects of intelligence, logical-mathematical and linguistic. As a result of Gardner's research, many people started to reconsider their definitions of intelligence. Presently, there is a growing recognition among educators, neuroscientists, psychologists and others that human beings possess a range of potentials and capacities that cannot be easily quantified.

In 1996, Daniel Goleman presented a more holistic view of intelligence in his famous book 'Emotional Intelligence' based on his own research as well as the research of many other scientists. Goleman argued that success in life depends more on the ability to manage emotions rather than simply mental abilities. He explained through research that having a high IQ does not necessarily guarantee success in life and many people with an ordinary IQ are more successful in their lives just because they are emotionally more intelligent.[15] According to Goleman, IQ measures are inadequate as determiners of an individual's future success (or happiness). Emotional intelligence, even though it is not a wholly quantifiable factor, is a more important contributor to an individual's potential success. The heart plays a major role in regulating our emotions and has a direct connection to emotional

14. Gardner, Howard (1985). *Frames of Mind: The Theory of Multiple Intelligences.* New York, Basic Books.
15. Goleman, Daniel (1995). *Emotional Intelligence.* New York, Bantam Books.

intelligence, even though that is not the only kind of intelligence that the heart possesses.

Emotional Intelligence of the Heart

Scientists of the past believed that the brain was the source of all emotions that we experience. It has been shown now that our emotions are much faster than our thought process and they surpass the linear reasoning process of the brain due to their speed. Since the thought processes of the brain are much slower than the speed with which emotions appear, emotions cannot be the result of a normal thinking process of the brain. Hence, as LeDoux showed in 'The Emotional Brain: The Mysterious Underpinnings of Emotional Life', it is not true that emotions originate in the brain.[16] The centre of the brain that plays the most important role in our emotional memory processing is called the amygdala. Recent research has shown that the heart affects this centre of the brain,[17] and thus our heart influences our emotion.

The concept of mind and body being distinctly separate entities originated when Rene Descartes (1596-1650), French mathematician and philosopher, proclaimed, "I think, therefore I am". Since then, philosophers have considered mind and body as separate entities, a concept known as Cartesian Dualism. Antonio Damasio, head of neurology at the University of

16. LeDoux, J. (1996). *The Emotional Brain: The Mysterious Underpinnings of Emotional Life*. New York, Simon and Schuster.
17. Armour, J. Andrew, M.D., Ph.D. & Ardell, Jeffry L., Ph.D. ed. (1994). *Neurocardiology*. New York, Oxford University Press.

To Buy !!

Iowa and a prominent researcher on human brain function, has recently challenged this premise in his book 'Descartes' Error: Emotion, Reason and the Human Brain'. Damasio showed that psychology's separation of reason from emotion is flawed and that emotions play a central role in human decision-making. He showed this through case studies of various patients whose own emotion-interpreting brain centres were damaged in accidents. Despite their perfect memory and no physical impairment, those individuals were lacking the ability to make correct decisions. Damasio showed that rational decisions are not the result of logic alone but they need the support of emotions and feelings.[18]

Intuition of the Heart

Intuition is an immediate knowing or learning of something without the conscious use of reasoning.[19] In other words, it is the process through which information is perceived by us which is normally outside the range of our conscious awareness. People use terms such as 'sixth sense' and 'gut feeling' to describe their intuitive feelings about a future event or a distant object. Often, the person having the intuitive feeling is certain about the experience and these feelings may be accompanied by positive emotions such as hope and excitement or negative emotions such as pessimism, fear or terror. People across all cultures generally know that our heart plays an important role in our sense of intuition. However,

---

18. Damasio, Antonio (1994). *Descartes' Error: Emotion, Reason and the Human Brain*. New York, Quill Publishers.
19. Webster's Dictionary

little scientific research has been conducted to elucidate the role of the human heart with respect to intuition.

One such study was recently conducted with the aim of showing, using the latest biomedical instruments, that the body has the ability to respond to an emotionally arousing stimulus seconds before it actually happens and also to investigate where and when in the body the intuitive information is processed.[20]

The results of this study found that both the heart and brain appear to receive and respond to intuitive information. A significantly greater heart rate deceleration (decrease in the rate of heart beat) was detected before the occurrence of future emotional stimuli as compared to future calm stimuli, showing that the heart plays a direct role in processing and decoding intuitive information. Another very interesting finding was that there appear to be significant differences in the way men process intuitive information as compared to the way women process the same kind of information. The results indicated that, in females, the heart was controlling the electrical signals in the cortex of the brain when the intuitive information was processed. Thus, "females are more attuned to information from the heart."[21] It is truly one of the signs of Allah that the ideal family unit is comprised of a balance between masculine intuition (brain-inclined) and feminine intuition (heart-inclined).

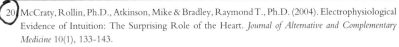

20. McCraty, Rollin, Ph.D., Atkinson, Mike & Bradley, Raymond T., Ph.D. (2004). Electrophysiological Evidence of Intuition: The Surprising Role of the Heart. *Journal of Alternative and Complementary Medicine* 10(1), 133-143.

21. Ibid

The Intelligence of the Heart
and the Intelligence of the Brain

The human brain works in a linear, logical manner. Its basic functions are to analyse, memorise, compartmentalise, compare and sort through the information obtained from our senses. Based on past information, experiences and memories, the brain sorts the incoming messages from our senses and transforms that data into perceptions, thoughts and emotions. This linear approach of the brain is necessary for our survival, but there are disadvantages to this ability. The brain can easily get stuck in a fixed pattern. This means that since there is already information in the head (it does not matter whether that information is based on reality or not), the brain always compares the new information to the old model it has and sees unconsciously if the new information matches with the old ideas and perceptions it has. This is the reason why it is so hard for us to change our old habits and perceptions.[22]

The German philosopher, Immanuel Kant (1724-1804) argued that intellect alone is totally inadequate for the comprehension of God's Essence.[23] That is true because the Qur'an says about Allah:

> There is nothing like unto Him. (Surah Ash-Shu'ara: 11)

The brain works by comparing new information with information that it already possesses. In the case of the Essence of Allah, the brain does not have anything to compare it with because there is

---

22. Childre, Doc & Martin, Howard (1999). *The HeartMath Solution*. New York, Harper San Francisco.
23. Kant, Immanuel, (1990). *The Critique of Pure Reason*. New York, Prometheus Books.

nothing like Allah. Therefore, the brain alone becomes helpless in discerning Allah directly. The only way it can understand Allah is by indirect knowledge - by contemplating upon the creations of Allah. That is why, Abu Bakr Siddique ﷺ said about the recognition of Allah:

> Glory to God who has not given to his creatures any other way to attain the knowledge of Him except by means of their helplessness and their hopelessness of ever reaching such attainment.[24]

The heart, however, cuts through any needless complexity or confusion, very similar to a flashlight beam that illuminates the darkness and allows one to see what is actually important. The intelligence of the heart processes incoming information in a different way that is less linear, more intuitive and more direct. In fact, there are many things in life, which we cannot explain logically. For example, belief in the Unseen and fear of Allah coupled with a desire to please Him all defy logic. But the heart can understand these concepts because of the way that it processes information.

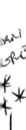

Imam Malik, the great jurist, referred to the superiority of the heart's intelligence over that of the brain when he described true knowledge:

> Knowledge does not refer to plenty of information; rather, knowledge is a light that Allah puts into the heart of a true believer.[25]

---

24. Ghazali, Imam Abu Hamid (1978). *Ihya Ulum ad Din*. Karachi, Darul Isha'at Publishers
25. Abu Zahra, Muhammad (1990). *Life of Imam Malik* (Urdu) Lahore, Sheikh Ghulam Ali & Sons.

Real knowledge is not the learning of facts and theories but the recognition of the Essence of Allah, the purpose of creation and the realisation of man's insignificance in comparison to the vastness of Allah's creation. It is this kind of intelligence which Rumi referred to in his poetic masterpiece *Mathnawi* as follows:

> "The intelligent person sees with the heart
> The result from the beginning;
> The one lacking in knowledge
> Only discovers it at the end."
> *(Mathnawi, Vol III, 4129)* [26]

The intelligence of the heart is of the humanistic type, which cares about other people as well. The intelligence of the brain is of a selfish kind, which is more concerned about its own survival. As researcher Dr. Paul Pearsall writes:

> "The brain itself never truly falls completely asleep. It has different levels of vigilance, but it never gives up its hold on the body…. The brain is mortality phobic." [27]

Psychologist Mihaly Csikszentmihalyi states in his book 'The Evolving Self' that our brain is inclined more towards pessimism and always expects the worst to happen. This is the brain's mechanism for being prepared for the unexpected. [28] It is this fear and pessimism of the human brain that is exploited by the shaytan when our heart wants to spend in the path of Allah:

[26] Rumi, Jalaluddin Mathnawi quoted in Helminski, Kabir (1999). *The Knowing Heart: A Sufi Path of Transformation*. Boston, Shambhala Publications.

27. Pearsall, Paul Ph.D. (1998). *The Heart's Code*. New York, Broadway Books.

[28] Csikszentmihalyi, Mihaly (1993). *The Evolving Self*. New York, HarperCollins.

Shaytan threatens you with poverty. (Surah Al-Baqarah: 268)

Similarly, shaytan takes advantage of the hidden fears of the brain and, as a result, the brain makes the heart spiritually sick as well. As a consequence, both the sinful brain and the sinful heart will be punished on the Day of Judgement:

> *Nay! If he ceases not, We will catch him by the Forelock (front portion of the brain), a lying, sinful forelock.* (Surah Al-'Alaq: 15-16)

> *The fire of Allah, kindled, which leaps up over the hearts.* (Surah Al-Humazah: 6-7)

While it is vital for man's survival on this earth to have intelligence of the brain, the possession of emotional intelligence is also important for happiness and success both in this world and in the Hereafter. For it is only people who have intelligent hearts who have been promised success in the next world:

> *The Day whereon neither wealth nor sons will avail, except him who brings to Allah a clean (sound) heart.* (Surah Ash-Shu'ara: 88-89)

Dr. Mohammad Iqbal, great Islamic poet, philosopher and Islamic scholar, in his 'Reconstruction of Religious Thought in Islam' made the following remarks about the heart:

> "The heart has a kind of inner intuition or insight which, in the beautiful words of Rumi, feeds on the rays of the sun and brings us into contact with aspects of Reality other than those open to sense-perception. It is, according to the Qur'an,

something which 'sees', and its reports, if properly interpreted, are never false."[29]

Relationship between the Heart and the Brain

Up until the 1970's, it was widely believed that the brain sends one-way commands to the heart which the latter then obeys. However, it was during the 1970's that it became clear that two-way communication exists between the heart and the brain.[30] When the brain sends a command to the heart through the nervous system, the heart does not always blindly obey but seems to use its own kind of logic. In addition, the research found that the heart was also sending messages back to the brain that the brain not only understood but also followed.[31]

More recent research is beginning to uncover specifically how the heart can communicate with the brain and it has been found that it can do so in four different ways.[32] [33] Firstly, the heart has its own set of 40,000 nerve cells or neurons that transmit information to the brain. This transmission of information through the nerves is called neural traffic and research has shown that the heart sends more neural traffic to the brain than the

29. Iqbal, Sir Mohammad (Allama) (1994). *The Reconstruction of Religious Thought in Islam.* New Delhi, Kitaab Bhavan.

30. Lacey, Beatrice C. & Lacey, John I. (1978). Two-Way Communication Between the Heart and the Brain: Significance of Time Within the Cardiac Cycle. *American Psychologist,* 99-113.

31. Lacey, Beatrice C. & Lacey, John I. Some autonomic-central nervous system interrelationships. In: Black, Perry. Ed. (1970). *Physiological Correlates of Emotion.* New York, Academy Press: pp. 205-227.

32. Childre, Doc & Martin, Howard (1999). *The HeartMath Solution.* New York, Harper San Francisco.

33. Ibid.

other way round.[34] Secondly, the heart has been found to secrete a very powerful hormone called Atrial Natriuretic factor (ANF) that has a profound effect on many parts of the body including those portions of the brain that are involved in memory, learning and emotions.[35] Thirdly, with every heartbeat, pressure waves are generated and when these travel through the arteries to the brain, there are recordable changes in the electrical activity of the brain.[36] Finally, the heart has an electromagnetic energy field 5,000 times greater than that of the brain and this field can be measured with magnetometers up to ten feet beyond the physical body.[37] Since the heart's energy field is greater than that of the brain, it can be assumed to have a profound effect on the brain's functions. It must be borne in mind that as the heart is the only organ in the body that pulsates so its effects will reach each part of the body at every moment.

Even though the timing of the heartbeat can be influenced by the brain (through the autonomic nervous system), the source of the heartbeat is present within the heart. There appears to be no need for nerve connections between the heart and the brain.[38] That is why, when a person has a heart transplant, all the nerve connections between the heart and the brain are cut but that does not stop the heart from working when it is placed in the new person's chest. [39]

34. McCraty, Rollin, Ph.D. (2003). *Heart-Brain Neurodynamics: The Making of Emotions*. Boulder Creek, California, Institute of HeartMath.
35. Cantin, Marc & Genest, Jacques (1986). The Heart as an Endocrine Gland. *Scientific American* 254(2), 76-81.
36. Childre, Doc & Martin, Howard (1999). *The HeartMath Solution*. New York, HarperSanFrancisco.
37. Pearsall, Paul Ph.D. (1998). *The Heart's Code*. New York, Broadway Books.
38. Childre, Doc & Martin, Howard (1999). *The HeartMath Solution*. New York, HarperSanFrancisco.
39. Ibid.

Usually, a person's heart is about the size of his own fist. As the body develops, the heart grows at the same rate as the fist. Hence, a baby's heart and fist are about the same size at birth. In the womb, however, that similarity is not always true. During the first few weeks after conception, the foetal heart occupies most of its mid-section. The ratio of the heart size to body size is nine times greater in the foetus than in the infant. It is common knowledge now that the heart of the unborn child develops and starts pumping long before the brain comes into existence. Even though the actual event which triggers the beating of the heart cells of a baby is not known, it is suspected as Paul Pearsall, Ph.D. writes, that "the mother's heart energy conveyed in primal sound waves contains the information that is the code that jump-starts our life."[40] Once the heart begins to beat, it continues to beat throughout a lifetime (auto rhythmic beating function) even when the brain stops working in cases like 'brain death'. Brain death is described as a condition when brain activity has stopped forever. Hence, even when the brain dies, the heart can still live. But when the heart dies (unless we find a replacement for the heart), the brain cannot live. Thus, the brain needs the heart for its survival more than the heart needs the brain.

The final words on this subject have been reserved for the verse of Iqbal highlighting the differences between the roles of the brain and the heart:

"Intellect (brain) one day said to the heart:
'I am a guide to those who have gone astray

---

40. Pearsall, Paul Ph.D. (1998). *The Heart's Code*. New York, Broadway Books.

Though bound to earth, I reach the heaven above
Just see how far reaching is my sway

I am cast in the mould of the legendary Khidhr
I am destined in the world to show the way

I am the interpreter of the book of life
I am an attribute of divine display

You are only a drop of blood
I am the envy of ruby's ray.'

'This is all true', replied the heart
'But look at me, be as it may
You look at life's trauma and drama
I see through life's white and grey

You deal with outer manifestations
And I am aware of the inner fray

Knowledge is to you, intuition to me
You seek God, I show how to pray

Limit of wisdom is restless doubting
I am cure for the malady of dismay

You are a lantern to illuminate a spot
I am a lamp to illuminate the path

You deal with time and space
I deal with Judgment Day

To what lofty place do I belong?
I am the pedestal of God Almighty, I say.'"

Aql aur Dil (Intellect and Heart) by Mohammad Iqbal [41]

41. Iqbal, Sir Mohammad (Allama) (1987). *Bang-e-Dara.* Lahore, Sheikh Ghulam Ali & Sons. English translation of the poem taken from: http://underprogress.blogs.com/weblog/2003/10/ intellect_and_h.html

CHAPTER THREE

The Unique Heart

HUMAN BEINGS ARE comprised of two components: body and soul (*ruh*). The Qur'an mentions that our body is made from the soil of this earth:

> *And among His signs is this, that He created you from dust.*
> (Surah Ar-Rum: 20)

Then, in this material being, Allah sends an angel to blow the spirit.

> *So when I have fashioned him and breathed into him (his) soul created by Me.* (Surah Saad: 72)

The reference to the dual nature of human beings is made in the Qur'an when Allah describes the creation of Adam:

> *I have created with Both My Hands.* (Surah Saad: 75)

The body and the soul undergo varying degrees of connection with each other and Ibn al-Qayyim al-Jawziya mentions the five stages of the body-soul relationship that span both our earthly and Eternal life:

1 Shortly after conception, Allah instils a *ruh* in the unborn child;
2 This connection continues when the child is born until the time of death;
3 During sleep there is partial disengagement of the soul from the body;
4 After death, in *barzakh*, although the soul has left the body, a connection still remains between the two;
5 On the Day of Judgement, souls and bodies will be re-united. The body-soul connection will be at its strongest then because in the Eternal Life there will be no sleep or death or any other physiological changes.[42]

Thus, the human body is made from earthly ingredients but the soul has heavenly origins. Therefore, there is a conflict between our material and spiritual being. The human body possesses desires similar to those of animals whereas the human soul strives for heavenly desires. This struggle ends with death, when the spirit leaves the body.

The instinct to worship is the desire of the human soul whereas instincts of hunger, thirst and sex are the desires of the body. Islam promotes a balance between the soul and the body, which is why it prohibits both monasticism as well as hedonism. All the ingredients of food for our physical body come from the soil of this earth because our physical being originated from this earth. However, since our soul was instilled by a heavenly being, its

---

42. Ibn al-Qayyim, al-Jawziya (1997). *Kitab ur-Ruh* (in Urdu). Lahore, Shabbir Brothers.

hunger is satisfied by the Divine. In fact, the food for our soul is the heavenly revelation of Allah – The Qur'an. The Qur'an is the spring of life for our soul.

In discussing the body-soul duality in the nature of human beings, Dr. Israr Ahmed, a contemporary Islamic scholar, medical doctor and commentator of the Qur'an, said the following:

> "The source of human volition and also the centre of the human soul is the heart. Human beings have a spiritual being as well as a physical being. The human soul is from Allah and it will return back to Allah as mentioned in the Qur'anic *ayah: 'Truly! To Allah we belong and truly, to Him we shall return.'* (Surah Al-Baqarah: 156). On the other hand, our physical body came from this world and it will return back to this world: *'Thereof (the earth) We created you, and into it We shall return you, and from it We shall bring you out once again.'* (Surah Ta-Ha: 55)

> The human heart is like a mirror between the two. The example of the heart is like a glass (*zujajah*), which contains a lamp (*misbah*) which is present inside a niche (*mishkat*) as described in Surah an-Nur (*ayah* 35). Our chest or ribcage looks similar to a niche; our heart is like a glass (*zujajah*) inside which the lamp of the soul is glowing." [43]

If the heart is not kept clean then the lamp of the soul is dimmed, much like a light-bulb that is covered with dust. However, if the heart is kept polished then the soul will light up the whole

43. Israr Ahmad, Dr. (2004). *Falsafa Siam-o-Qiam-e-Ramadan* (Urdu Lecture). Lahore, Anjuman Khuddamul Qur'an.

human being. This light or *nur* was most apparent in Prophet Muhammad ﷺ. The Prophet ﷺ gave the following advice for polishing the heart:

> There is a polish for everything that takes away rust; and the polish for the heart is the remembrance of Allah. *(Bukhari)*

There are three types of self or states of spiritual development that have been mentioned in the Qur'an. The lowest of these is called *nafs ammarah* (12:53), the self that is prone to evil. *Nafs lawwamah* (75:2) is the self that feels conscious of doing evil, resists, repents and tries to amend. The highest stage of all is *nafs mutma'innah* (89:27) which is when the self achieves full peace and happiness. Our objective is to control *nafs ammarah* that urges us to fulfil our baser instincts with no thought for the consequences and ultimately achieve the inner peace that comes with *nafs mutma'innah*.

This can only come about when we obey Divine commands and live our lives according to Islamic teachings. There is more wisdom in these commandments than we can ever fully comprehend but our limited knowledge is slowly allowing us to understand and appreciate some of these as the following passages show.

The Heart and *Salah* (Prayer)

During our everyday life, the brain is in a physically higher position than our heart and that sometimes results in the arrogance of the brain. However, when we prostrate to Allah as in *salah*, our heart attains a higher position in our body than our brain and that is the state of a human being in which he/she is closest to Allah. This is emphasised both in the Qur'an and in the hadith:

> *Fall in prostration and draw near to Allah!* (Surah Al-Alaq: 19)

> The closest a slave ever is to his Lord is when he is in prostration, so make much supplication. *(Muslim)*

Islam places even greater emphasis on congregational worship and the reasons for this become apparent in the light of scientific evidence.

Heart cells are similar to other cells in the rest of the human body in terms of chemical composition. However, there is one thing that heart cells do differently from other body cells that makes them unique – they are the only cells in the body to pulsate or beat rhythmically.

In the laboratory, if a single heart cell is placed on a slide and observed under a microscope, it continues to beat for a short while, then loses its rhythm and dies. Similarly, if two heart cells are placed on a slide at a distance, they also die after a short time of beating without rhythm. However, if two heart cells are placed close together on a slide (they do not need to touch each other), they start beating in synchrony (with the same rhythm) and they do not die. The same phenomenon occurs on a larger scale in the case of a complete heart. All the heart cells beat in synchrony (with the same rhythm in unity), which makes the heart such a powerful organ.

What is the reason behind the synchronous beating of the two heart cells (even though they are not connected to each other), which prevents them from dying? Each tiny heart cell produces waves of electromagnetic energy as it pulsates. According to Joseph Chilton Pearce, author of 'The Biology of Transcendence', when the electromagnetic waves produced by two heart cells on a slide match (synchronise), the two heart cells strengthen each other and start to beat in unity.[44] This phenomenon can be observed on a macroscopic (larger) level as well. When people are in close proximity in a room, their hearts start to beat with the same rhythm. Even their breathing pattern synchronises in such instances.

This phenomenon, called 'entrainment', was first observed in the seventeenth century by a European scientist called Christian Huygens with pendulums. When there are many pendulums swinging close to each other, they will end up swinging in synchrony with the largest pendulum no matter how different their rate of swinging to start with.

As mentioned previously, the heart produces waves of electromagnetic energy. In fact these can be measured using magnetometers from as far as three feet away from the body. When people are in close proximity, their electromagnetic waves interact with each and this interaction can also be measured using sensitive instruments. This means that all the hearts in a given space start to be affected by the waves generated by the strongest heart (which could be the heart of the leader) and start to beat

44 Pearce, Joseph Chilton (2002). *The Biology of Transcendence*. Rochester, Vermont, Park Street Press.

with the same rhythm (pulled into entrainment) as that of the strongest heart.[45]

When the companions of Prophet Muhammad ﷺ were sitting in his presence, they used to remember Allah much more than when they were alone. Since the heart of Prophet Muhammad ﷺ was always engaged in the remembrance of Allah (his heart was awake even when his eyes were asleep), his heart would pull the hearts of his companions in entrainment.[46]

When Muslims are praying behind one Imam and they straighten their rows, as a result, their hearts become synchronised. Their hearts beat in unity and, thus, are strengthened. This is the wisdom behind a hadith narrated by Nu'man bin Bashir from Prophet Muhammad ﷺ according to which he used to tell his companions before the *salah*:

> Straighten your rows three times. Otherwise, Allah will make your hearts turn against each other. *(Abu Dawud)*

The Heart and *Dhikr* (Remembrance of Allah)

Allah has made the heart and all the other parts of the human body for His remembrance. The heart is pacified by the remembrance of Allah (*dhikr*) and good deeds:

> *Verily, in the remembrance of Allah do hearts find rest.* (Surah Ar-Ra'd: 28)

---

45. Childre, Doc & Martin, Howard (1999). *The HeartMath Solution.* New York, HarperSanFrancisco.
46. Yusuf, Hamza (ISNA 1999) *Putting the Heart into Worship* (audio speech). Hayward, Alhambra Productions.

Commenting on the Islamic *dhikr*, Louisa Young, a British journalist and author, writes in *The Book of the Heart:*

> "The simple pulse, the beating of the drum of the heart, is the repetitive rhythm which leads and propels meditation – the voyage into the heart – in all religions....
>
> One Muslim ritual is the recitation of the Qur'an; the flowing, hypnotic rhythm of the Arabic words has often been compared to the heartbeat. Grief caused by the separation from God is assuaged by remembering God: 'Verily in the remembrance of Allah do hearts find rest.' This remembrance is *dhikr* – remembrance, the mental and verbal repetition of a verse of the Qur'an or one of the names of God."[47]

In fact, it has been scientifically shown that the human heart is responsive to *dhikr*. One such study, conducted at the Akbar Clinics in the US, examined the response of the body when listening to the recitation of the Qur'an. The heart rate, blood pressure and muscle tension were monitored among three groups of volunteers – Muslims who understood Arabic, Muslims who did not understand Arabic and non-Muslims who did not understand Arabic.

The results of the study show very clearly that listening to the recitation of Qur'an results in the relaxation of smooth muscles, reduction of the heart rate and all the physiological changes that are indicative of release from stress and anxiety. These effects were

---

[47] Young, Louisa (2003). *The Book Of The Heart*. New York, Doubleday.

produced both among Muslims and non-Muslims, regardless of whether they understood the Arabic language or not.

Interestingly, different *ayat* of the Qur'an produced different effects among all the subjects of the study. For example, the recitation of those verses promising reward (verses of *targheeb*) had a greater stress-reducing effect on the listeners whereas listening to the recitation of the verses promising punishment (verses of *tarheeb*) had less of a stress-reducing effect on the listeners. [48]

A similar scientific study, conducted at the University of Khartoum in Sudan, looked at the effect of Qur'anic recitation on patients with hypertension (high blood pressure). The results of this study also showed that listening to the recitation of the Qur'an contributed significantly to a lowering of blood pressure among the patients.[49]

In the light of this research, it is therefore not surprising that the companions of Prophet Muhammad ﷺ used Qur'anic *dhikr* to heal medical conditions. Listening to the Qur'an recited beautifully can have a healing effect which is why the Prophet ﷺ emphasised:

> Beautify the Qur'an with your voices. *(An-Nasa'i and Abu Dawud)*

---

48. Elkadi, Ahmed, Health and Healing in the Qur'an in Athar, Shahid, M.D., Ed. (1993). *Islamic Perspectives in Medicine - A Survey of Islamic Medicine: Achievements & Contemporary Issues.* Indianapolis, American Trust Publications.

49. Badri, Malik (2000). *Contemplation: An Islamic Psychospiritual Study.* London, The International Institute of Islamic Thought.

The Heart and *Tawaf* (Circumambulation of the Ka'bah)

Performing the *tawaf* is one of the most spiritually uplifting times in the life of a Muslim. It is done in an anti-clockwise manner with the left side of the body facing the Ka'bah. The same anti-clockwise motion can also be observed in nature from the largest scale to the smallest scale. For example, all the planets in our solar system revolve around the sun in an anti-clockwise manner, while electrons also rotate around the nucleus of an atom in the same way.

Some Islamic scholars have said that *tawaf* is performed in an anti-clockwise manner because in this position the heart (which is towards the left side of the body) is inclining towards the Ka'bah.[50] The human soul, because of its heavenly origins, yearns to meet Allah and so the heart, as the seat of the human soul, inclines towards the Ka'bah symbolising that desire. The Ka'bah also symbolises the Islamic concept of Monotheism. During *tawaf*, Muslims testify that Allah is the centre of existence and He is the focus of our hearts.

The Heart and the Acceptance of Islam

The heart plays a central role in the acceptance of Islam, whether it is a non-Muslim who embraces Islam or a born-Muslim who endeavours to better understand his faith. Blaise Pascal, the seventeenth century French scientist and religious philosopher, once said about the human heart:

---

50. Yusuf, Hamza (2004). *Diseases of the Heart: Signs, Symptoms and Cures of the Spiritual Diseases of the Heart*. Chicago, Starlatch Press.

"The heart has its reasons the mind will never know. Those on whom God has imparted religion by intuition are very fortunate and justly convinced." [51]

In this oft-quoted statement, Pascal was referring to intuition of our heart. According to Pascal, religious truth is often known through intuition. We have seen evidence, in the previous chapter, to show that females are more heart-inclined and that intuition in females relies more on the response from the heart. It may be for this reason that eighty percent of those who accept Islam are women. It should be clarified that the decision to accept Islam is not based on mere emotion because almost all of these women stay steadfast on their decision to accept Islam until their death.

One of these many women converts is Jeanette Hablullah, a doctor of neuropathy from America, who chose Islam after many years as a Catholic. In her book about the heart, 'The Magnificent Organ', she describes the human heart not only as a vital organ and a physical entity but also as the source of judgement and wisdom.[52] She also explains that a pious and God-fearing heart heals our bodies and souls.

Allah took a pledge from all souls before their birth regarding His Existence and Authority as the Qur'an states:

And (remember) when your Lord brought forth from the Children of Adam, from their loins, their seed (or from Adam's loin his offspring)

---

51. Clouser, Roy (1999). *Knowing with the Heart: Religious Experience & Belief in God.* Downers Grove, IL, InterVarsity Press.

52. Hablullah, Jeanette, ND (2002). *The Magnificent Organ: The Heart of Qur'an, Hadith, Science and Wholistic Healing Experiences.* Columbia, MO, Olive Media Services.

and made them testify as to themselves (saying): "Am I not your Lord?" They said:""Yes! We testify," lest you should say on the Day of Resurrection: "Verily, we have been unaware of this." (Surah Al-A'raf: 172)

Almost immediately afterwards is the following *ayah*:

And surely, We have created many of the jinns and mankind for Hell. They have hearts wherewith they understand not, they have eyes wherewith they see not, and they have ears wherewith they hear not (the truth). They are like cattle, nay even more astray; those! They are the heedless ones. (Surah Al-A'raf: 179)

It is not mere coincidence that the Qur'an speaks of the heart as an organ of intellect after mentioning the covenant taken by all human souls. This implies that our hearts carry the primordial memory of our covenant with Allah taken from our souls. In other words, every child is born with a natural belief in Allah and an inclination to worship Him alone, which is called *fitrah*. However, the environment in which a person is brought up then affects that natural state as the Qur'an asks of the non-believers:

Do they not then think deeply in the Qur'an, or are their hearts locked up (from understanding it)? (Surah Muhammad: 24)

Dr. Mohammad Iqbal, famous Islamic philosopher and poet, raised the very pertinent point that regardless of the strength of logical evidence provided, in the matter of accepting Islam, it is the heart that must be touched. He said to one of his students:

"According to my understanding, the human heart and brain process information in different ways. The brain may sometimes reject many strong proofs and does not care about them. But the heart on the other hand may be impressed by a small incident and, all of a sudden, the whole life pattern may change. The matter of acceptance of Islam is related to the heart much more than the brain. The actual thing, which an Islamic preacher (*da'ee*) should know, is what are the things that touch the heart of non-believers. We have many mental proofs to testify the truth of Islam but we have very few 'hearty proofs'…. In the acceptance of Islam, the heart is the actual thing. When the heart agrees on a change and it is convinced about a matter, then the whole body has no choice except to obey the heart."[53]

So the matter of accepting or rejecting Divine Guidance depends upon the heart more than the brain. When the heart opens to the truth, the whole body follows it. As Allah says in the Qur'an:

And whomsoever Allah wills to guide, He opens his breast to Islam, and whomsoever He wills to send astray, He makes his breast closed and constricted, as if he is climbing up to the sky. (Surah Al-An'am: 125)

This point is well illustrated by an incident (one of many) that took place at the time of the Prophet Muhammad ﷺ as narrated by Ibn al-Qayyim al-Jawziyah in his book *Zad al-Ma'd*:

"After the conquest of Makkah, the Prophet was circumambulating the house when Fudala ibn 'Umayr decided

---

53. Khan, Wahiduddin (1994). *Tablighi Tahreek*. New Delhi, Al-Risala Books.

to kill him. He drew near to him. The Prophet said, "Fudala?"
He replied, "Yes! Fudala, O Messenger of Allah!" He said,
"What were you saying to yourself?" "Nothing!" He said, "I was
invoking Allah!" The Prophet laughed then said, "Ask Allah for
forgiveness!" Then he placed his hand on his chest and there was
peace in his heart. Fudala used to say later on, "By Allah! By the
time he took his hand off my chest, none of Allah's creation was
dearer to me than him! As I was returning to my family I passed
by a woman I used to converse with, she said, "Come over!" I
said, "No, Allah will not allow it, nor will Islam!"" [54]

Not only does the individual heart play a vital role in embracing
Islam, but Muslims as a whole need strong hearts to be united as
an *ummah*, as a hadith states:

12,000 Muslims united (as one heart) cannot be defeated.
(Abu Dawud)

Commenting on the underlying wisdom of this hadith, Jeanette
Hablullah, writes:

"We have gatherings greater than this in some cities here in
the United States at least twice a year but where is our effect?
Our hearts have not yet reached the necessary level. The heart
must first purify and right the individual in which it resides,
then it will join with other purified and righteous hearts. When
this happens, there is nothing in this universe that can have a
sufficient opposing force." [55]

54. Ibn al-Qayyim, al-Jawziya (1997). *Zad al-Ma'd*. Karachi, Nafees Academy.
55. Hablullah, Jeanette, ND (2002). *The Magnificent Organ: The Heart of Qur'an, Hadith, Science and Wholistic Healing Experiences*. Columbia, MO, Olive Media Services.

Maulana Mahmood-ul-Hasan, who was imprisoned on the Island of Malta by the British government in India, said that during his years in prison, he contemplated over the cause of the decline of the Muslim nation and he reached the following conclusion:

"There appear to be two reasons for the decline of the Muslim *ummah* today:
  i Muslims have forsaken the Qur'an; and
  ii Muslims are disunited." [56]

Today the defence system (immune system) of the Muslim *ummah* has become very weak. One of the features of a healthy body with a good defence system is that the antibodies (defence army of the body) learn from the past. When they encounter a virus or any other harmful intruder in the body, they remember it and so if it enters the body again, these antibodies unite to defend the body from the onslaught. If a virus is present in four persons and only one person falls ill, it is not the virus that is to blame but the immune system of the ill person. Similarly, the Muslim *ummah* should work to build up its own strength before placing the blame for our illness elsewhere.

Imam Shafi has rightly said in one of his poetic verses:

"We blame time and the fault is in us,
There is no fault in time except us."
(Diwan ash-Shafi)

---

56. Israr Ahmed, Dr. (1994). *Jamaat Sheikh ul Hind & Tanzeem-e-Islami* (Urdu). Lahore, Anjuman Khuddamul Qur'an.

The companions of Prophet Muhammad ﷺ had very strong immunity and a good defence system and their hearts were united because they had vaccinated themselves with the Qur'an. The remedy for the current situation that the Muslim *ummah* finds itself in is quite simply a daily dose of the Qur'an and Sunnah.

And hold fast, all of you together, to the Rope of Allah (i.e. this Qur'an) and be not divided among yourselves. (Surah Al-Imran: 103)

If you differ in anything amongst yourselves, refer it to Allah and His Messenger (i.e. Qur'an and Sunnah) (Surah An-Nisa: 59)

I am leaving with you two things. If you hold them tight, you will never go astray. They are the Book of Allah (Qur'an) and my Sunnah (Hadith). *(Muslim)*

When we stop competing with each other with wealth and material possessions; when we sacrifice our egos and learn to tolerate differences of opinions within the boundaries of the Qur'an and Sunnah, then our hearts will unite, and with that unity will come an unparalleled strength. As the old saying goes – 'United we stand and divided we fall'.

Umar bin al-Khattab ؓ, the second rightly guided caliph, said:

There is no Islam without a congregation and there is no congregation without a leadership.[57]

---

57. Israr Ahmed, Dr. (1994). *Jamaat Sheikh ul Hind & Tanzeem-e-Islami.* Lahore, Anjuman Khuddamul Qur'an.

Allah reminds us in the Qur'an that we can only be brothers in faith when our hearts are united:

> *And remember Allah's favour on you, for you were enemies and He joined your hearts together, so that by His Grace, you became brethren (in Islamic faith).* (Surah Al-Imran: 103)

The Heart and the Mother-Child Bond

By the time an unborn child is four and half weeks old in the womb of the mother, its sense of hearing (auditory system) is complete and it can hear sounds produced in the body of the mother. Of all the sounds that the child hears in the womb, the most predominant one is the continuous rhythmic sound of its mother's heartbeat. As long as the mother's heartbeat is normal and regular, the unborn child feels safe. However, if the mother is in a prolonged heightened state of anxiety then this will have adverse effects on the unborn child. In the 1940's, Lester Sontag, M.D. first discovered that the mother's heartbeat affects the heartbeat of her unborn child.[58] This is why it is so important for the mother and those around her to take care of her emotional well-being as well as her physical health.

The unconscious memory of the mother's heartbeat in the womb remains with the child after birth and throughout his/her life. Thomas Verny, M.D., in his book 'The Secret Life of the Unborn Child', has mentioned that it is because of the

---

58. Bernard, J. & Sontag, L. (1947). Fetal Reactions to Sound. *Journal of Genetic Psychology* 70, 209-210.

unconscious memory of the mother's heartbeat that a baby can be comforted by being held close to someone's chest in much the same way that many adults can fall asleep to the steady sound of the ticking of a clock.[59]

It is known that when our heart waves and our brain waves match (synchronise), our body functions at "optimum capacity".[60] Similarly, when the wave-frequencies of the hearts of mother and baby are synchronised, as Joseph Chilton Pearce puts it, "the mother's developed heart furnishes the model frequencies that the infant's heart must have for its own development in the critical first months after birth." [61] One of the times that this synchronisation of the mother-child heart waves occurs is when the mother is breast-feeding her child.

During breast-feeding, the child is close to the mother's heart and listens to her heartbeat. As Joseph Chilton Pearce writes, "On holding her infant in the left-breast position with its corresponding heart contact, a major block of dormant intelligences is activated in the mother, causing precise shifts of brain function and permanent behaviour changes."[62] Perhaps this could be why most mothers instinctively place their babies to their left breast, keeping those hearts in proximity. The importance of close body contact, or better yet, close heart-to-heart contact of the mother and her newborn is stressed by James W. Prescott, Ph.D. of the Institute of Humanistic Science:

59. Verny, Thomas M.D. & John Kelley (1981). *The Secret Life of the Unborn Child*. New York, Dell Publishing Co., Inc

60. Childre, Doc & Martin, Howard (1999). *The HeartMath Solution*. New York, HarperSanFrancisco.

61. Pearce, Joseph Chilton (2002). *The Biology of Transcendence*. Rochester, Vermont, Park Street Press.

62. Pearce, Joseph Chilton (1992). *Evolution's End*. New York, HarperSanFrancisco.

"Only in the human mammal do we find the newborn separated from its mother at birth and the mother not breastfeeding her newborn and infant. We have discovered that such aberrant behaviours which violate millions of years of evolutionary biology and psychobiology have exacted a terrible price upon the physical, emotional and social health of the newborn and infant and as a child, adolescent and adult – depression, impulse dyscontrol, violence and substance abuse." [63]

Mother's milk contains just the right amount of fatty acids, lactose, water and amino acids for digestion, brain development and growth. It also contains many types of immunities a baby needs in early life while his/her own immune system is maturing. In addition, human milk contains the lowest concentration of fats and proteins compared to the milk of other mammals. This makes feeding of the newborn necessary after about every twenty minutes. In contrast, rabbit milk has such a high concentration of fat and protein that the mother need only feed the baby rabbit once a day. Such low frequency feeds are found in all other mammals. The fact that human milk is poor in nutrients and is digested quickly makes it necessary for the mother to breast-feed her baby several times day and thus make frequent contacts which are beneficial for both mother and baby.

It is precisely for these reasons that in the Qur'an, Allah has emphasised the importance of breast-feeding and has set the time period for breast-feeding at two years:

---

63. Prescott, James W. (Spring 1997). Breastfeeding: Brain Nutrients in Brain Development for Human Love and Peace. *Touch The Future* Newsletter.

And We have enjoined on man (to be dutiful and good) to his parents. His mother bore him in weakness and hardship upon weakness and hardship (during pregnancy), and his weaning (stopping of breast-feeding) is in two years - Give thanks to Me and to your parents - unto Me is the final destination. (Surah Luqman: 14)

CHAPTER FOUR

Diseases of the Heart and Their Cures

The Day whereon neither wealth nor sons will avail, except him who brings to Allah a clean heart (Qalb saleem). (Surah Ash-Shu'ara: 88-89)

THIS *AYAH* CLEARLY refers to the spiritual heart, although it is important to remember that the spiritual heart resides within the physical heart and the two are closely interconnected.

Spiritual diseases of the heart can have a negative impact on the physical heart and indeed the rest of the body. So, treating spiritual diseases of the heart will have a positive impact on the physical heart and body. Laboratory experiments at the HeartMath Institute have shown that when people focus on their hearts and activate a core heart feeling such as love, care or appreciation, this focus changes their heart rhythms immediately. When positive emotions such as happiness, compassion, care and appreciation are activated, there is increased production of dehydroepiandrosterone (DHEA) in the body, a hormone that fights aging in human beings. If the heart suffers from spiritual diseases such as envy, anger or hate, DHEA production is reduced and the production of the stress hormone cortisol is increased, resulting in aging and reduction of potential life span. It is little wonder, therefore, that the Prophet ﷺ often used to make the supplication:

> "O Allah! I seek refuge in you from anxiety (stress) and grief, weakness and laziness, miserliness and cowardliness, the burden of debts and from being overpowered by men." *(Bukhari, Abu Dawud and At-Tirmidhi)*

Similarly, the actions taken to control the diseases of the physical heart will also have a positive effect on the spiritual heart.

This chapter starts by looking at the physical diseases of the heart and their cures according to the Qur'an and Sunnah, and then addresses the more important matter of how to attain a sound heart free from spiritual stains and defects (*qalb saleem*) by treating various spiritual diseases.

Physical Diseases of the Heart

Among the physical diseases of the heart, the major one is coronary heart disease. This occurs when the arteries that supply the heart with blood and oxygen become narrowed because of deposits of cholesterol on the artery walls. If not enough oxygenated blood can reach the heart then an angina attack results. In more severe cases, if the supply of blood is completely cut off from a portion of the heart, a heart attack will result. Coronary heart disease is one of the major causes of death in the Western world. According to statistics, about one million people in the US[64] and

---

64. Athar, Shahid, M.D. (1995). *Health Concerns for Believers: Contemporary Issues.* Chicago, Kazi Publications, Inc.

110,000 people in the UK[65] die each year from coronary heart disease. Although modern medicines and heart surgery can treat coronary heart disease, the best course of action is prevention through lifestyle changes.

The vast majority of diseases are related to our diet and the Islamic lifestyle as prescribed by Prophet Muhammad ﷺ is an ideal course of prevention for many diseases, including those of the heart. Prophet Muhammad ﷺ disliked excessive eating. He lived with a flat belly and he died with a flat belly. He is reported to have said:

> No man fills a vessel worse than his stomach. A few morsels are enough for the son of Adam (human being) to keep his back upright. But if he must eat more, then he should fill one third of his stomach with food, one third with drink and leave one third empty for the air (for easy breathing). *(At-Tirmidhi)*

It is important to exercise moderation in our eating habits. Limiting the consumption of food results in a tender heart, a strong intellect, a humble self and it weakens desires. Excessive eating brings about the opposite of these praiseworthy qualities. Ibrahim ibn Adham said:

> "Anyone who controls his stomach is in control of his deen, and anyone who controls his hunger is in control of good behaviour. Disobedience towards Allah is nearest to a person who is satiated with a full stomach, and furthest away from a person who is hungry." [66]

---

65. Department of Health, UK.
66. Ghazali, Imam Abu Hamid (1978). *Ihya Ulum ud Din.* Karachi, Darul Isha'at Publishers.

Two of the most important aspects of Islam are *salah* and *dhikr* and these are equally important as part of a healthy lifestyle as the Prophet Muhammad ﷺ advised:

> Dissolve and digest your food through the process of remembrance of Allah and offering of prayers. *(Abu Nuaym)*

It is for this reason that the five obligatory prayers are arranged as they are. Traditionally, the Dhuhr and 'Isha prayers are offered after a meal and these are longer, allowing us to gently exercise the body and prevent us from sleeping immediately after meals. The wisdom behind this was explained by the Prophet ﷺ:

> Do not go to bed immediately after the meals; it will harden your heart. Avoid any hard or large quantum of exercise immediately after meals; it will also cause damage. *(Abu Nuaym)*

The quality of the food we eat affects both our physical and spiritual health. It is important to eat pure food that has been obtained using *halal* income. In Surah Al-Kahf, when the Sleepers of the Cave[67] awoke after their long sleep and sent one of their number to the nearby town market to buy some food, they advised him to get food which they described as *'Azka ta'aman'* (pure food). These pious young men realised the importance of eating pure food in order to maintain a pure heart.

Part of the reason that the hearts of Muslims are destroyed is because we are no longer careful about choosing food that is pure.

---

67. A group of five to seven pious young men who had fled the persecution of a tyrant ruler and hid in a cave and Allah put them to sleep for about 300 years.

Instead of eating homemade food filled with *barakah*, we prefer fast food, which in the words of Sheikh Hamza Yusuf, is "made with haste and waste, two attributes of the devil."[68] It is important for us to be conscious of purity of the food we are eating for the sake of the physical and spiritual health of our hearts.

Types of Spiritual Heart

The heart is the midpoint between the body and soul. During our earthly life, there is a continual struggle between the desires of the body and those of the soul. If the heart inclines more towards the passionate desires of the body, it first becomes veiled, then it is hardened and finally it becomes diseased. Conversely, if the heart inclines more towards the desires of the soul, it starts to receive spiritual power that strengthens it. According to the Qur'an, people have three kinds of hearts spiritually:

1 *Mu'min* (believer in Oneness of Allah) - somebody whose heart is alive.
2 *Kafir* (disbeliever in Allah) - somebody whose heart is dead.
3 *Munafiq* (hypocrite) - somebody whose heart has a disease.

The disease of hypocrisy is considered to be worse than disbelief as the *munafiq* tries to deceive Allah.

While the heart of the *mu'min* is clear and alive, it is always vulnerable to attack from envy, backbiting, arrogance and other spiritual diseases. Sheikh Ibn Taymiyyah in his book 'Diseases of

---

68. Yusuf, Hamza (2001). *Agenda to Change Our Condition*. Hayward, Zaytuna Institute.

the Hearts and Their Cures' quotes from Ali bin Abi Talib ؓ, about the different kinds of spiritual hearts:

> "The hearts are of four types: the clear heart that is illuminated by a torch - this is the heart of the believer. The encased heart - this is the heart of the disbeliever. The inverted heart - this is the heart of the hypocrite. And, the heart that has two attractions, a time when it is called to faith, and a time when it is called to hypocrisy - these are a people that have mixed good actions with evil ones."[69]

Importance of the Science of *Tazkiyyah* (Purification of the Heart)

Islam is not merely a religion but a complete code of life. The injunctions of Islam dealing with the outward aspects of our life form the science of *fiqh* (jurisprudence), while the commandments of Islam dealing with the inward aspects of our personalities are described in the science of *tazkiyyah* (purification of the heart). *[For further details, see Appendix II]*

Allah's purpose in sending Prophets and Messengers to humankind and revealing religious scriptures has been *tazkiyyah* (purification) of people's hearts. The Qur'an mentions the purpose of the Prophethood of Musa ﷺ as purifying the hearts of his people:

> *Go to Pharaoh, verily, he has transgressed all bounds. And say to him: 'Would you purify yourself.' And that I guide you to your Lord, so you should fear Him?* (Surah An-Na'ziat: 17-19)

---

69. Ibn Taymiyyah, Sheikhul-Islam (2003). *Diseases of the Hearts and Their Cures*. Birmingham, Dar us-Sunnah Publishers.

Prophet Ibrahim ﷺ prayed for a Prophet who would purify his own people:

Our Lord! Send amongst them a Messenger of their own, who shall recite unto them Your Verses and instruct them in the Book (this Qur'an) and 'Al-Hikma', and purify them. Verily! You are the All-Mighty, the All-Wise. (Surah Al-Baqarah: 129)

Allah accepted Ibrahim's ﷺ du'a and bestowed Prophethood on one of his progeny, Muhammad ﷺ, whose purpose has also been described in the Qur'an:

Similarly We have sent among you a Messenger of your own, reciting to you Our Verses and purifying you, and teaching you the Book (i.e. Qur'an) and the 'Hikma' (i.e. Sunnah), and teaching you that which you used not to know. (Surah Al-Baqarah: 151)

Indeed, Allah purified the heart of the Prophet Muhammad ﷺ so that he could receive the Qur'an in an incident which can be considered as the first heart surgery. *[See Appendix I for further details]*

The reason that *tazkiyyah* is so important is that it is a pre-requisite for success in the Hereafter:

Indeed he succeeds who purifies his own self. And indeed he fails who corrupts his own self. (Surah Ash-Shams: 9-10)

Ibn Abbas, the great interpreter of the Qur'an and Companion of Prophet Muhammad ﷺ is reported to have said: "Prophet Muhammad ﷺ taught us Iman first and then he taught us the

Qur'an."[70] The seed of Iman is planted in the heart and the heart must be spiritually strong for Iman to grow.

Spiritual Strength of the Heart

The first step towards strengthening the spiritual heart is to contemplate the purpose of our creation, our relationship to Allah, our accountability to Allah on the Day of Judgment and the ways we can rectify our self, by concentrating on our heart. Frequent remembrance of death makes this life distasteful for us and we are less likely to follow those desires that lead us to disobey Allah. If we indulge too much in this world, our hearts are likely to be adversely affected. Dr. Iqbal writes about this condition in his book 'Reconstruction of Religious Thought in Islam':

> "In our constant pursuit after external things we weave a kind of veil around the appreciative-self which thus becomes completely alien to us. It is only in the moments of profound meditation, when the efficient-self is in abeyance, that we sink into our deeper self and reach the inner centre of experience." [71]

Similarly, Ibn Ata illah Iskandari, the great Egyptian saint and scholar, in his book *Al-Hikam ul Ata'iyah* mentioned:

> "If we do not get upset whenever we miss an act of virtue or prayer and if we do not feel shame after committing an act of

---

70. Israr Ahmed, Dr. (1993). *Renaissance of Islam: The Real Task Ahead*. Lahore, Anjuman Khuddamul Qur'an.
71. Iqbal, Sir Mohammad (Allama) (1994). *The Reconstruction of Religious Thought in Islam*. New Delhi, Kitaab Bhavan.

disobedience to Allah then that is a sign of the death of our (spiritual) heart." [72]

In the same way that our physical body depends on food for its nourishment, so our spiritual heart depends upon Iman, acts of virtue and prayer for its well being. Spiritual diseases are dangerous for the health of the heart and, if left untreated, can result in its death.

Animals have only a very rudimentary understanding of right and wrong, while human beings have been endowed with *Al-Furqan* (the criterion to judge between right and wrong).

And the soul and Him Who perfected it in proportion. And then showed him (inspired with conscience of) what is wrong for him and (what is) right for him. (Surah Ash-Shams: 7-8)

This is accompanied by a highly developed capability to feel shame and guilt, which is again unique to humans. These qualities mean that human beings are capable of almost angelic behaviour. However, if a human being does not feel shame or guilt upon disobeying Allah, then the heart of that person is dead and his behaviour becomes worse than that of an animal. Such human beings who do not differentiate between right and wrong are described in the Qur'an as cattle:

They are like cattle, nay even more astray; those! They are the heedless ones. (Surah Al-A'raf: 179)

---

72. Iskandari, Ibn Ata illah (1984). *Al-Hikam ul Ata'iyah* (Urdu title: Ikmal-ush-Shiyam; translated by Khalil Ahmed Siharanpuri). Karachi, Idarah Islamiyat.

The ultimate goal of the purification of our heart is to reach the stage of having what the Qur'an calls *'Qalb Saleem'* (a sound heart). This is the kind of heart about which Rumi noted:

> "If the heart is restored to health
> And purged of sensuality,
> then *the Merciful God is seated on the throne.*
> After this, He guides the heart directly,
> Since the heart is with Him."
> *(Mathnawi, Vol I, 3665-66)* [73]

The heart intuitively knows what is wrong because according to a tradition of Prophet Muhammad ﷺ narrated on the authority of Wabisa bin Mabad ؓ who came to the Messenger of Allah:

> You have come to ask about righteousness?" I said: "Yes." He said: "Consult your heart. Righteousness is that about which the soul feels tranquil and the heart feels tranquil, and wrongdoing is that which wavers in the soul and moves back and forth in the breast (in your heart) even though people again and again have given you their opinion in its favour." *(Ahmad and Ad-Darimi)*

Similarly, in another hadith narrated by Nawas bin Sam'an, Prophet Muhammad ﷺ is reported to have said:

> Virtue is good ethics and behaviour and wrong action is what irritates the heart and you do not desire other people to see it. *(Muslim)*

---

73. Rumi, Jalaluddin Mathnawi quoted in Helminski, Kabir (1999). *The Knowing Heart: A Sufi Path of Transformation*. Boston, Shambhala Publications.

Hence, the heart is not only an organ of consciousness but also an organ of conscience (having the ability to differentiate between right and wrong). Therefore, in situations where there are no clear injunctions of Qur'an, Sunnah, *fiqh* (jurisprudence) or *Ijma'a* (consensus of Islamic scholars on an issue), the only option is for *mu'mins* to allow their hearts to guide them in these matters; the heart will feel at peace with the truth and uneasy with falsehood. [74]

In discussing the education of the heart, Kabir Helminski, states:

"The heart is not merely a vague metaphor for some undefined capacity for feeling. The heart is an objective cognitive power beyond intellect. It is the organ of perception that can know the world of spiritual qualities. It is the heart that can love, that can praise, that can forgive, that can feel the Majesty of God...

But the human heart in most cases has suffered so much artificial conditioning that it has become a distorted and distorting instrument. In order for the heart to be an adequate cognitive instrument, it needs reconditioning. The reconditioning of the heart is a task that must be guided by objective principles." [75]

The principles that we need to use have been given to us by our Creator in the form of the Qur'an and Sunnah.

O mankind! There has come to you a good advice from your Lord (i.e. the Qur'an, ordering all that is good and forbidding all that is evil),

---

74. Ibn Rajab, Hanbali (1995). *Jami al-Uloom wal Hukam* (Commentary on An-Nawawi's Forty Ahadith) (Urdu language). Lahore, Al-Faisal Publishers & Booksellers.
75. Helminski, Kabir (1999). *The Knowing Heart*. Boston, Shambhala Publications.

and a healing for that (disease) in your breasts - a guidance and a mercy for the believers. (Surah Yunus: 57)

These must be put into practice on a daily basis in order to educate, purify and rectify our hearts.

Spiritual Diseases of the Heart and their Cures

Verily Allah does not look to your faces and your wealth but He looks to your heart and to your deeds. *(Muslim)*

We will be held responsible for our actions on the Day of Judgement and so it is our responsibility to refrain from sinful acts during our time here on Earth. Shaytan does not have access to the thoughts that enter our hearts. However, he does have the ability to whisper into our hearts to tempt us away from the Straight Path:

(Shaytan) who whispers in the breasts of mankind. (Surah An-Nas: 5)

A spiritually healthy heart will find it relatively easy to resist the whisper of shaytan. However, a weak heart will find this more difficult to resist and so the whisper of shaytan is very strong and effective in misguiding a weak-hearted man. Shaytan has used the same techniques to lead man astray from the beginning of time and they have been effective ever since because human nature remains fundamentally unchanged as Maryam Jameelah eloquently expresses:

"Man's disposition, his biological and psychological needs, his physical and mental capacities, the temptations which make him succumb to evil and his eternal quest for the moral and spiritual values that give human life its meaning and purpose and distinguishes him from the lower animals, have not changed at all since the emergence of homo sapiens!" [76]

Because of this lack of originality on shaytan's part in manipulating us, it becomes somewhat easier to understand the ways in which we are deceived by shaytan to fall into his trap and to diagnose the spiritual diseases of the heart.

The heart, as with every other organ in the body, has a specific function, which if carried out correctly is a sign of its health. The function of the heart is to know its Creator and to seek the pleasure of Allah. If the heart fails in this function, then it is sick and diseased.[77]

The diseases of the heart, according to Ibn al-Qayyim al-Jawziya, can be divided into two major categories:
1. Diseases of *Shubahat* (doubts)
2. Diseases of *Shahawat* (desires) [78]

The disease of *shubahat* creeps into the heart when Iman is lowered and creates a sense of anxiety and restlessness which then governs our actions:

---

76. Jameelah, Maryam (1981). *The Generation Gap: Its Causes & Consequences.* Lahore, Mohammad Yusuf Khan & Sons.

77. Ghazali, Imam Abu Hamid (1978). *Ihya Ulum ad-Din.* Karachi, Darul Isha'at Publishers.

78. Ibn Rajab Hanbali, Ibn Qayyim & Ghazali (1989). *The Purification of the Soul.* U.K., Al-Firdous Publications Ltd.

...whose hearts are in doubt that ask your leave. So in their doubts they waver. (Surah At-Tawbah: 45)

It comes about because of a lack of complete trust (*tawakkul*) in Allah and a lack of understanding about His Divine Decree (*Qadr*). The spiritually healthy heart has firm belief in Allah, submits to His Divine Decree and harbours no doubt.

The disease of *shahawat* arises when the heart succumbs to the desires of the self in excess of its needs. For example, eating, sleeping and talking to excess are all diseases of desire.

The Qur'an succinctly tells us in Surah al-Asr what the general treatment is for these two categories of disease. For the disease of doubt, the treatment is to have firm belief in the truth:

And (the believers) recommend one another to the truth. (Surah Al-Asr: 3)

For the disease of desire, it is recommended that we have patience to control these desires:

And (the believers) recommend one another to patience.
(Surah Al-Asr: 3)

In this section, some of the major spiritual ailments of the heart will be discussed and some suggestions about their cures will be presented. It should be pointed out here that owing to the vastness of this subject, this book represents just a drop in the ocean on the subject of *tazkiyyah*. As the Punjabi spiritual poet, Sultan Mohammad Bahoo, said:

"Hearts are deeper than rivers and oceans,
Who knows all the secrets of the heart."

Corruption of the Heart through the Ears and Eyes

The eyes and ears provide information from one's environment
that is then processed by the heart which in turn governs our
actions. It follows therefore that our actions will be influenced
by what we hear and see around us and that we should exercise
some control over what we feed these senses.

Verily! The hearing, and the sight, and the heart, of each of those you
will be questioned (by Allah). (Surah Al-Isra: 36)

Our sense of hearing is circular, while our sense of sight is linear.
In other words, we can hear sounds from all directions but we can
only see what is in front of us. If we are confronted by something
distasteful, we can protect our eyes by simply closing them, but
to protect our ears, we must physically leave that place. Similarly
our sense of hearing (as opposed to our sense of sight) remains
active even in the dark and while we are sleeping. In the story of
the cave dwellers (*Ashab-ul Kahf*), Allah tells us that He covered
their sense of hearing so that their sleep would not be disturbed:

Therefore We covered up their (sense of) of hearing (causing
them, to go into a deep sleep) in the Cave for a number of years.
(Surah Al-Kahf: 11)

Hence, it is more difficult to protect the ears from corruption in comparison to the eyes. It is important therefore, to pay attention to what we listen to and protect ourselves from those sounds which will corrupt the heart. This includes all bad speech, undesirable language and backbiting regardless of whether it is through the media or in the company we keep.

Many of us are unaware of the harmful effects of listening to some types of music on the heart. We are surrounded by music each time we leave the home in department stores, shops and blaring out of cars. While there is little that we can do about this, we can, however, take responsibility for what we bring into our homes. Much of the music available nowadays has inappropriate and suggestive lyrics and is designed to excite us.

All music has the ability to move the heart and penetrate the soul. Worthless and lewd music with the use of instruments diverts the heart from the remembrance of Allah and can even awaken dormant desires within the heart, which can lead to wrong actions. Similarly, melody that praises and glorifies Allah or narrates the virtues of the Prophet ﷺ can awaken the desire towards worship. This type of music does not use instruments (except perhaps the *daff* or drum) to excite or arouse passions.

The purest sound that the ears can listen to is that of The Holy Qur'an recited in a melodious voice. It brings peace to the anxious heart, tranquillity to the restless heart, comfort to the aching heart and inspiration for the yearning heart. It is all things to all people and should be made a regular practice in our daily lives.

It is equally important for the health of the heart for us to guard the sight as mentioned in the Qur'an:

> *Tell the believing men to lower their gaze and guard their modesty. That is purer for them. Verily, Allah is All-Aware of what they do. And tell the believing women to lower their gaze and guard their modesty and not to show off their adornment except only that which is apparent.*
> (Surah An-Nur: 30-31)

When we gaze at any sight that appeals to us, we become attracted to it and the image of what we see becomes imprinted on our heart. If the sight is prohibited then the imprinted image will pollute the heart. It has been reported that the Prophet ﷺ once said to his companions:

> The glance is a poisoned arrow of shaytan. Whoever lowers his gaze for Allah, He will bestow upon him a refreshing sweetness which he will find in his heart on the day that he meets Him.
> *(Ahmad)*

We must be careful to distinguish between reality and illusion. Often we are presented with altered or distorted images in the media that make things appear more beautiful than they really are. Our hearts may yearn to be like the people we see on screen or to achieve their lifestyle and acquire their possessions. We begin to display the symptoms of *al-wahn* (the love of this world and dislike of death) and experience the dissatisfaction that accompanies it. Big screens, sophisticated sound systems and state-of-the-art special effects all come together to create an illusion which seduces the viewer. Soon we are addicted to these images and more time is spent watching television and DVDs than on any other activity. It is our responsibility to protect ourselves and our families from the damage done through the media by limiting what we bring into our homes. It is not necessary to have multiple televisions, cable channels, satellite dishes, Hollywood and Bollywood videos and DVDs, Playstations and computer games.

There is a hadith that states that angels do not enter homes in which there are pictures.[79] It follows, therefore, that we deprive ourselves of the mercy of angels if we keep our TV switched on for most of the day and night.

Corruption of the Heart through the Tongue

> "The tongue is a great endowment from Allah; though small in size, its crime is enormous." [80]

So said Imam Ghazali, centuries before it was known that the tongue is the strongest muscle in the human body. The ability of human beings to speak and articulate distinguishes them from all other animals:

> He (Allah) created man. He taught him eloquent speech.
> (Surah Ar-Rahman: 3-4)

The tongue has the greatest potential to be used for good – to praise Allah, to encourage others in good deeds, to heal rifts. However, it has an equally great potential to be destructive

---

79. "Angels do not enter a house which has either a dog or a picture in it." (Bukhari).
80. Ghazali, Imam Abu Hamid (1978). *Ihya Ulum ad-Din*. Karachi, Darul Isha'at Publishers.

through backbiting, obscene and misleading talk, hypocrisy, boasting, quarrelling, singing, lying, mocking etc. all of which can affect and ruin a person's heart. The Prophet ﷺ said:

> The faith of a servant is not put right until his heart is put right, and his heart is not put right until his tongue is put right. *(Ahmad)*

Abu Huraira ﷺ reported that Ibn al-Abbas said:

> A person will not feel greater fury or anger for any part of his body on the Day of Judgment more than what he will feel for his tongue, unless he only used it for saying or enjoining good. [81]

The following story illustrates how important the heart and the tongue are. Luqman was a wise man from Africa and was bestowed great wisdom by Allah with regards to the Qur'an. He spent the early part of his life as a slave and his master was a good and intelligent man. The master deduced that Luqman was no ordinary man and thus set him a task to test his intelligence. One day, Luqman's master ordered him to slaughter a sheep and to bring the worst part of it to him. Upon slaughtering the sheep, Luqman brought to his master the heart and tongue of the animal.

A few days later, Luqman was again instructed by his master to slaughter a sheep, but this time he was asked to bring the best part of the animal to him. Upon slaughtering the sheep, Luqman again brought to his master the heart and tongue of the animal. The master asked Luqman how the same organs could be the best

---

81. Ibid.

and worst parts. The wise Luqman explained that the tongue and the heart are the sweetest parts of the body if the owner is pure; but that they can also be the worst parts of the body if the owner is evil.

The following sections highlight the most common faults of the tongue that we are guilty of and how to rectify these.

Unnecessary Speech *(Fudhool ul Kalam)*

The root cause of many problems is unnecessary and excessive speech and this distracts us from the remembrance of Allah as related in the following hadith on the authority of Ibn Umar:

> Do not talk excessively without remembering Allah, because such excessive talk without the mention of Allah causes the heart to harden, and the person furthest from Allah is a person with a hard heart. *(At-Tirmidhi)*

Words are like arrows; once they have been fired, they cannot be taken back and it is very hard to undo the damage that has been done. We can never know just how far-reaching the effects of our words can be as the following hadith narrated by Abu Huraira ﷺ highlights:

> The servant speaks words, the consequences of which he does not realise, and for which he is sent down into the depths of the Fire further than the distance between the east and the west. *(Bukhari)*

Not only is vain and excessive talk bad for our spiritual health, it is also injurious to our physical health. James J. Lynch, M.D., a U.S. researcher and scientist, has found through 20 years of scientific research that speech affects our whole body especially the cardiovascular system and raises the blood pressure.[82] For those people that have an existing condition of high blood pressure, talking can exacerbate their condition to a dangerous level.[83] On the other hand, when we listen, our blood pressure decreases.

It is also worth pointing out here that excessive laughter is also bad for the spiritual health of the heart as the Prophet ﷺ is reported to have said:

> Do not laugh too much for too much laughing deadens the heart. *(Ibn Majah)*

The best way to refrain from vain and idle speech is to engage the tongue in the remembrance of Allah (*dhikr*) as much as possible. It is an excellent way to become closer to Allah and to achieve rest and peace of the heart, while repelling the whisperings of shaytan. When the tongue is occupied with the remembrance of Allah, it cannot engage in evil acts that will displease Allah and may hurt our fellow human beings. Thus, *dhikr* can also act as a shield from the fire of hell.

---

82. Lynch, James J. (1985). *The Language of the Heart: The Body's Response to Human Dialogue.* New York, Basic Books, Inc.
83. Lynch, James J. (Aug.1996). Why Listening is Good for You. *Readers Digest,* 122-124.

Backbiting *(Ghibah)*

Backbiting *(ghibah)* is a sinful practice that is prevalent in many societies and involves talking about someone in their absence in a manner that would hurt their feelings if they were to hear it, even if it is the truth. If a falsehood is said about someone in their absence, then this is the sin of calumny *(buhtan)*. Backbiting is strictly prohibited in the Qur'an and Sunnah, while calumny is an even more serious crime as it involves lying and backbiting.

> When a group of companions asked Prophet Muhammad ﷺ about backbiting *(ghibah;* gossip), he explained clearly that backbiting *(ghibah)* refers to mentioning something about your Muslim brother that he hates. The Prophet was asked, "What if that thing I mentioned was something truthful about him?" The Prophet said, "If it was in him, then you have committed backbiting *(ghibah)*, and if it was not in him, then you have committed *al-buhtan*" - which is a sin more enormous than backbiting. *(Muslim, Abu Dawud and At-Tirmidhi)*

In the Qur'an, Allah says:

> *And spy not, neither backbite one another. Would one of you like to eat the flesh of his dead brother? You would hate it (so hate backbiting). And fear Allah. Verily, Allah is the One Who accepts repentance, Most Merciful. (Surah Hujurat: 12)*

Here, backbiting is likened to eating the flesh of one's dead brother – an act which is repulsive to all of us. A dead person cannot defend or protect himself and by eating his flesh, his person is being violated. Similarly, in the case of backbiting, the absent person cannot defend himself while his honour and reputation are being sullied.

Backbiting occurs when people do not have control over their tongues or they are bored so they pass the time by engaging in gossip about other people. However, Islam encourages us to mind our own affairs and not involve ourselves with that which does not concern us:

> One of the merits of a person's Islam is his abandoning what does not concern him. *(At-Tirmidhi)*

Sitting in a place where other people are backbiting while we listen is the equally grave sin of 'passive backbiting'. We must stop it if we have the authority to do so or at least leave the offending gathering as politely as possible. We are often afraid to speak out against the bad for fear of ridicule, but we must remember that the Qur'an instructs us to '*enjoin the good and forbid the evil...*' (3:110) and this can be done in a gentle manner as the following story illustrates. An Islamic scholar was invited to dinner one evening where he overheard two people engaged in backbiting at the dinner table. He turned to them and said, "Brothers, it is interesting that most people start their dinner with bread but you two have started your dinner by eating the flesh of your dead brother!"

As brothers and sisters in Islam we have a duty of care to one another and this is eloquently expressed in the following hadith:

> A believer is a mirror to his brother. A believer is a brother of a believer: he protects him against any danger and guards him from behind. *(Al-Adab al-Mufrad and Abu Dawud)*

A mirror shows the exact nature of someone without exaggeration at a particular point in time. It does not flatter or degrade. When a person leaves the mirror, the image disappears; it is not retained in the mirror for others to see. Similarly, when we meet our Muslim brothers and sisters, we should not speak in terms of excessive flattery or humiliate them. Once we have parted company we should not retain any ill feeling towards them within us and we should not engage in talking about them behind their back. If we hear others doing so, we have a duty to protect our fellow brothers and sisters in their absence. For if we do so, then Allah will protect us:

> The Muslim who helps another when the latter's honour and dignity are under attack, shall be helped by Allah, Glorious and Sublime is He! – at a time when he would wish for Allah's help. But he who forsakes a Muslim whose dignity is under attack, shall have Allah forsake him at a time when he would wish for Allah's help. [84]

Lying *(Kizb)*

One of the most serious faults of the tongue is that it can be used to tell lies. Abdullah ibn Massoud quotes the Prophet ﷺ as saying:

---

84. Ghazali, Imam Abu Hamid (1978). *Ihya Ulum ud Din.* (Kitab Adaab al Suhbah) Karachi, Darul Isha'at Publishers.

Maintain truthfulness, for truthfulness leads to righteousness, and righteousness leads to Heaven. A man continues to maintain truthfulness until he is recorded in Allah's book as truthful. Refrain from lying, because lying leads to blatant evil, and evil leads to the fire. A man continues to lie until he is recorded in Allah's book as a liar. *(Bukhari, Muslim, Abu Dawud and At-Tirmidhi)*

A lie is a most serious crime because it can be used to cover up other evil actions such as adultery, theft and murder. If the liar is successful in doing this once, then he gains the confidence to continue to behave in this way until he is weighed down by his evil actions. It is for this reason the hadith says that lying leads to blatant evil. A persistent liar is not only recorded in Allah's book as a liar but he also loses his respect in the sight of his fellow human beings – a very humiliating situation.

Conversely, if a person is honest at all times then there is no opportunity for him to cover other shameful deeds and thus truthfulness leads to righteousness. Truthfulness and honesty encompass many aspects of speech and thought. The most obvious is to refrain from telling lies. In addition, we should not make promises that we have no intention of fulfilling and once we do make a promise, we should be careful to fulfil it regardless of how trivial it may seem.

Most hateful it is with Allah that ye say that which you do not do.
(Surah As-Saff: 3)

Moreover, the truthful person will be respected by his fellow human beings and recorded as a truthful person in the eyes of Allah – a most honourable situation.

The following advice of the Prophet ﷺ related by Abu Huraira ؓ sums up beautifully how we should behave with regard to the tongue:

> Let whoever believes in Allah and the Last Day either speak good or remain silent. *(Bukhari)*

Anger *(Ghadhab)*

Anger is a self-defence mechanism given to human beings, but unless it is properly controlled, it becomes a very destructive quality. Prophet Muhammad ﷺ explained the origin of anger:

> Anger is from shaytan and shaytan has been created from fire. Since water extinguishes fire, therefore, when one of you is overtaken by anger let him make wudu. *(Abu Dawud)*

Fire is a beneficial commodity for us as long as it is under control. However, it is chaotic by nature and can easily get out of control. It is at this point that it becomes destructive. Another feature of fire is that it rises in the upward direction, unlike dust which is attracted downwards. So the natural state of shaytan is to be arrogant while the natural state of humans is to be humble. However, when we are angry, we tend to take on the shaytanic quality of arrogance.

The best of you are those who are slow to anger and swift to cool down...Beware of anger, for it is a live coal on the heart of the descendants of Adam. *(At-Tirmidhi)*

The Prophet ﷺ was the perfect example of this as mentioned in the Qur'an:

And by the Mercy of Allah, you (O Muhammad ﷺ) dealt with them gently. And had you been severe and harsh-hearted, they would have broken away from about you; so pass over (their faults), and ask (Allah's) Forgiveness for them. (Surah Al-Imran: 159)

Anas bin Malik ﷺ was the personal servant of Prophet Muhammad ﷺ for the last ten years of the Prophet's life. He said that during that time, the Prophet did not scold him once. If Anas ever made a mistake, the Prophet would always be smiling.

Anger is like an intoxicant which clouds the senses and under whose influence a person may commit other more serious crimes. The angry person has no control over what he says and may say things that can cause harm to others and that he later regrets. It is very important therefore not to let this emotion overcome us in the first place as the Prophet ﷺ once advised a man who came to him:

Abu Huraira ﷺ reported that a man came to the Prophet ﷺ and said to him: "Advise me!" The Prophet ﷺ said, "Do not become angry and furious." The man asked (the same) again and again, and the Prophet said in each case, "Do not become angry and furious." *(Bukhari)*

If we do find ourselves becoming angry then we should change our environment, for example by leaving the room, or our position (from standing to sitting or lying) and we should make *wudu* (ablution) or drink some water to cool down the fire of anger.

It is a noble quality to be able to control anger and to hold the tongue even when we are overcome with emotions. As the saying goes: "A moment of patience at the time of anger saves one from years of regret and sorrow".

Love of this world and Dislike of death *(Al-Wahn)*

When a large number of individual Muslims suffer from a particular spiritual disease, then it reaches epidemic proportions and the whole *ummah* becomes afflicted. We are currently in the grip of just such a disease and that is love of this world and dislike of death *(al-wahn)*. The root cause of the love of this world is greed and the cause for dislike of death is fear.

If we look honestly at our lives then we find that we spend much of our time in pursuit of wealth and accumulation of material possessions. Indeed, Allah knows all too well about our nature and says in the Qur'an:

> *The mutual rivalry for piling up of worldly things diverts you. Until you visit the graves (i.e. till you die). Nay! You shall come to know, Again, Nay you shall come to know. Nay! If you knew with a sure knowledge (the end result of piling up, you would not have occupied*

yourselves in worldly things). Verily, You shall see the blazing Fire (Hell)! And again, you shall see it with certainty of sight! Then, on that Day, you shall be asked about the delight (you indulged in, in this world). (Surah At-Takathur: 1-7)

The desire to accumulate has diverted us away from our remembrance of death and the Hereafter. For what purpose will our accumulation have served when we are in our graves? In a tradition narrated on the authority of Thawban, the Prophet ﷺ said:

> The nations will summon each other against you as those eating summon each other to their dish. Someone asked, "Will that be because of our small numbers at that time?" He replied, "No, you will be numerous at that time: but you will be froth and scum like that carried down by a torrent (of water), and Allah will take the fear of you from the breasts (hearts) of your enemy and cast *al-wahn* into your hearts." Someone asked, "O Messenger of Allah, what is *al-wahn*?" He replied, "Love of the world and dislike of death."
> *(Abu Dawud and Ahmad)*

The symptoms of this disease are the desire to gain money, power, fame and status. Yet we have not yet grasped how dangerous this disease can be for our heart.

> Two hungry wolves in a herd of sheep are not as destructive and harmful as the love of the money and extravagance are for the religion of a person. *(At-Tirmidhi)*

It is important to realise that materialism is completely superficial. There is nothing that the materialistic way of life can offer to nourish and pacify the human soul. In fact, even the physical pleasure of acquiring something is short-lived and we are soon absorbed by the desire to acquire something else which is bigger or better. In short, we are never satisfied.

> Narrated Hakim bin Hizam: I asked the Prophet (for some money) and he gave me, and then again I asked him and he gave me, and then again I asked him and he gave me and he then said, "This wealth is (like) green and sweet (fruit), and whoever takes it without greed, Allah will bless it for him, but whoever takes it with greed, Allah will not bless it for him, and he will be like the one who eats but is never satisfied. And the upper (giving) hand is better than the lower (taking) hand." *(Bukhari)*

> Narrated Ibn 'Abbas: I heard the Prophet saying, "If the son of Adam (human being) had two valleys of money, he would wish for a third, for nothing can fill the belly of Adam's son except dust, and Allah forgives him who repents to Him." *(Bukhari)*

The first step towards treating the disease of *al-wahn* is to sincerely repent to Allah and ask Him to bestow *barakah* on all that we have. Secondly, the Prophet ﷺ recommended that we visit the graves[85] in order to diminish our love of this world and to serve as a reminder of death. When we ultimately leave this world we will only take with us our balance of good deeds and the reward of the following three things: [86]

---

85. Ibn Majah
86. Reported by Abu Huraira (Muslim)

a Recurring charity
b Knowledge by which people benefit
c The prayers of our children

Therefore, our limited time on earth should be spent amassing good deeds to the best of our ability, fulfilling both the rights of Allah and of our fellow human beings. We should also invest our time in actions that will help us and others once we have passed away. The greatest legacy we can leave is to ensure that our children are given a sound Muslim education and that they set aside the time to pray for us when we have passed away rather than spend their time in pursuit of wealth.

It is also worth spending some time examining all the possessions that we have. We will find that we do not need as many things as we have and we do not need to replace them as often as we do. We should be content with what we have (which is a great deal). What is important is not how much we have but how much *barakah* there is in what we do have.

Sociologists in the West have identified a disease which they term 'reference anxiety'. This arises when we constantly compare what we have with others and find what we have to be lacking. It always helps to look at people who have less material possessions than us rather than at those who have more. This will help us to appreciate what we have and realise that we do in fact have far more than we deserve, yet we are still not grateful.

Abu Huraira reported that the Messenger of Allah ﷺ said, "Look at those who are lower than you and do not look at those who are higher than you. That is more likely to prevent you underestimating the blessing of Allah on you." *(Muslim)*

There is great dignity in simplicity as exemplified by our Beloved Prophet ﷺ. He did not have many material things, but he was well-respected and loved for his strength of character. We should try to emulate him as our role model rather than be seduced by the superficial beauty of this world.

> Abu 'Abbas Sahl ibn Sa'd as-Sa'idi said, "A man came to the Prophet ﷺ and said, 'Messenger of Allah, show me an action for which Allah will love me and for which people will love me if I do it.' He said, 'Do with little of this world and Allah will love you, and do with little of what belongs to other people and people will love you.'" *(Ibn Majah)*

Stinginess *(Bukhal)*

Stinginess or miserliness is another spiritual disease of the heart, from which the Prophet ﷺ taught us to seek Allah's refuge. Stinginess originates from selfishness and greed and occurs when we withhold what we have been blessed with from others, in the mistaken belief that we will be poorer. The Prophet ﷺ said of stinginess:

> Be aware of stinginess. It destroyed many nations before you. It made them to shed the blood of each other and misappropriate what was sacrosanct. *(Muslim)*

The nature of the Muslim is to be generous; generous with his time, his wealth and his efforts in the Path of Allah and in helping his fellow human beings. The best cure for the disease of stinginess is to spend in the way of Allah as this will connect the heart with Allah.

> *By no means shall you attain Al-Birr (piety, righteousness, etc.), unless you spend (in Allah's Cause) of that which you love; and whatever of good you spend, Allah knows it well.* (Surah Al-Imran: 92)

The heart is always inclined towards that on which it has spent the most. If we spend on the material possessions of this world, then our hearts are inclined towards this world. Conversely, if we spend in the way of Allah, the heart will incline towards Allah and seek to earn his pleasure. In the words of Prophet Isa عليه السلام:

> Give your wealth to your Lord, because your heart stays wherever your wealth stays. [87]

Many Muslims believe that if they have paid their *zakat* then they have spent in the way of Allah. *Zakat* is an obligatory welfare contribution which is incumbent on every capable Muslim annually. If we wish to purify our hearts then we must sacrifice more than the minimum amount set forth by Islamic Law. We must also give *sadaqah* on a regular basis. The Prophet ﷺ said:

> Sadaqah extinguishes sin as water extinguishes fire.
> *(At-Tirmidhi)*

---

87. Islahi, Amin Ahsan (2002). *Tazkiyyah Nafs.* Faisalabad, Malik Sons Publishers.

Sadaqah appeases the Lord's anger and averts an evil death.
(At-Tirmidhi)

Any good deed that we do selflessly for the benefit of others and for the pleasure of Allah is considered *sadaqah*. When we give in this way, it does not decrease what we have but increases it as Allah has promised in the Qur'an:

> *The likeness of those who spend their wealth in the Way of Allah, is as the likeness of a grain (of corn); it grows seven ears, and each ear has a hundred grains. Allah gives manifold increase to whom He pleases. And Allah is All-Sufficient for His creatures' needs, All-Knower.*
> (Surah Al–Baqarah: 261)

It is worth reflecting on the fact that we have a great deal of disposable income for unnecessary superficialities in life yet when it comes to spending in the way of Allah, we have neither the time nor the money to give. If we all sincerely wished for our fellow human beings what we would wish for ourselves, then we could go a long way towards eradicating poverty and misery in this world. The next time we feel we cannot give up of our wealth in the path of Allah then it is worth remembering the following words of the Prophet Muhammad ﷺ:

> Stinginess and iman can never be together in the heart of a believing servant. *(An-Nasa'i, Ahmad, Al-Hakim and Bukhari)*

Showing Off *(Riyaa)*

Showing off is regarded as 'hidden idolatry' *(al-shirk al-khafiyy)* in Islamic teachings. It refers to a desire to show off and seek praise from others. It takes away sincerity and seriousness from the act of virtue a person is performing and his actions become superficial. Empty actions without sincere intentions are worthless and can lead a person to the ultimate disease of hypocrisy *(shirk)*. Abu Sa'eed al-Khudri narrates that Prophet Muhammad ﷺ said:

> Shall I not tell you what I fear for you more than *al-Masih ad-Dajjal?*" They replied: "Yes." He said: "It is hidden *shirk (riyaa)* such as when a person stands in prayer and he improves his prayer when he knows that others are watching. *(Ahmad)*

The danger of ad-Dajjal (the anti-Christ) is confined to a specific time, while the danger of *riyaa* is present at all times and places. Because the intention of a person is hidden so the disease of *riyaa* is not always apparent.

It is a common human weakness to enjoy being praised, which is why Rumi said that animals gain weight by eating fodder whereas the human *nafs* (ego) becomes fat through the ears, meaning that the human ego becomes inflated by listening to its own praise.[88] It is important to remember that any deeds carried out with the intention of being seen by others will not incur any reward. The following hadith narrated by Abu Huraira highlights the severity of this:

---

88. Akhtar, Maulana Hakeem Mohammad (n.d.). *Sermons on Divine Love (Muwa'iz dard-e-Mohabbat).* Karachi, Kutab Khana Mazhari.

I am Independent of all the partners (ascribed to me). Whoever performs a deed while associating partners with Me, I will leave him and his *Shirk*. *(Muslim)*

The best cure for the disease of *riyaa* is to check the intention *(niyyah)* before performing any action. As a believer, our goal should be only to please Allah because:

To our Lord (Allah) is the End. (Surah An-Najm: 42)

Arrogance *(Takkabur)*

Arrogance *(takabbur)* stems from egotism and overestimation of oneself and one's abilities or merits. 'To arrogate' means to make an unjust claim to something. An arrogant person makes an unjust claim of his abilities or merits, which in reality have been granted to him by Allah. He also shows his pride by humiliating others. In Islam, arrogance has been condemned very strongly both in the Qur'an and the hadith:

And turn not your face away from men with pride, nor walk in insolence through the earth. Verily, Allah likes not each arrogant boaster. (Surah Luqman: 18)

One will not enter Paradise, if one has an atom's weight of arrogance in his/her heart. *(Muslim and At-Tirmidhi)*

Arrogance was the reason that Shaytan did not bow down to Adam 🕮 when asked to by Allah, and was consequently expelled from Paradise.

(Allah) said: "What prevented you (O Iblis) that you did not prostrate, when I commanded you?" Iblis (shaytan) said: "I am better than him (Adam), You created me from fire, and him You created from clay." (Allah) said: "(O Iblis) get down from this (Paradise), it is not for you to be arrogant here. Get out, for you are of those humiliated and disgraced." (Surah Al-A'raf: 12-13)

Pharaoh was arrogant and refused to believe in Allah even after signs and miracles were shown to him by Prophet Musa ﷺ. Pharaoh said to his people, *'I am your Most High Lord.'* Therefore, God seized him with punishment. (Surah An-Naziat: 24-25)

Arrogant persons are deluded into thinking that they are better than other people. They believe that their qualities (power, intelligence, wealth) are self-made and will stay with them forever. They do not realise that these are bounties from Allah who has the power to take those blessings away within the blinking of an eye. Allah describes their state of mind in the Qur'an:

Thinks he that none can overcome him? He says (boastfully): "I have wasted wealth in abundance!" Thinks he that none sees him? (Surah Al-Balad: 5-7)

Another type of arrogance is called *Ujb* which is a state in which a person suffers from self-admiration of his abilities and merits. *Ujb*, in itself, is a destructive vice, which ruins faith and actions and is a product of self-love or narcissism. *Ujb* can apply to both good and bad actions. A virtuous person may become conceited about his good deeds. Similarly, a doer of wicked deeds may feel proud of his actions, both of which are wrong.

The opposite of arrogance is humility and it is this quality that we must nurture in our hearts to the extent that there is no room for arrogance.

> And the slaves of the Most Beneficent (Allah) are those who walk on the earth in humility... (Surah Al-Furqan: 63)

We can learn lessons from the Qur'anic accounts of those people who were arrogant and their hapless fate, such as Pharaoh and Qarun. We can also gain a great deal by reading accounts of the Prophet ﷺ who was a most humble man. At the time of the conquest of Makkah, he entered the city as the head of the army of 10,000 people, he was riding a camel and, out of humility, he had bowed down so much that his forehead was touching the hump of his camel.

Attending congregational prayers and performing Hajj will emphasise how insignificant and ordinary we are in relation to all of Allah's creation. We are all servants of Allah and are completely dependent on Him for our being and existence. When we stand on the Plain of Arafat along with millions of other Hajis, we all stand humbled before Allah in the same garments and there is no way of knowing who is a king and who is a pauper. We will all stand this way on the Day of Judgement accompanied by nothing but our deeds. It is a sobering and life changing experience for those whose hearts are open to it.

Envy *(Hasad)*

Envy *(hasad)* or jealousy is a disease of the heart in which a person resents what another person has and desires it for himself. It is without doubt one of the most corrosive of all human emotions. Helmut Schoeck, a German sociologist, in his book entitled 'Envy: A Theory of Social Evolution', believes that a society's "civilizing power of achievement" depends on how well it controls envy.[89] While modern materialistic society does nothing to curb this emotion, religion provides the solution to control its destructive effects. Prophet Muhammad ﷺ advised:

> Abstain from envy (jealousy). Indeed, envy finishes all the good acts and their rewards as the fire does away with firewood. *(Abu Dawud)*

The destructive nature of envy is mentioned in the Qur'an:

> *Say: I seek refuge with the Lord of the Day-break. From the evil of what He has created. And from the evil of the darkening (night) as it comes with its darkness. And from the evil of the witchcrafts when they blow in the knots. And from the evil of the envier when he envies.* (Surah Al-Falaq: 1-5)

History is rich with examples of envy that have lead to major crimes. The first murder in human history occurred because of envy. Qabil, the son of Adam ﷺ, was jealous that Allah had accepted the sacrifice of his brother Habil. As a result, Qabil murdered Habil. Similarly, the stepbrothers of Prophet Yusuf

---

89. Schoek, Helmut (1969). *Envy: A Theory of Social Behaviour.* Indianapolis, Liberty Press.

ﷺ were jealous of their father's love for him. Blinded by their feelings of envy, the stepbrothers of Yusuf ﷺ conspired to kill him by throwing him into a well and abandoning him and then lying to their father about the incident.

When we look at the blessings given to other people by Allah, our own self (*nafs*) becomes dissatisfied with our present condition. Instead of being grateful to Allah for what He has blessed us with, we resent and begrudge what other people have. This in turn leads us to commit other crimes to satisfy our own sense of justice. However, we should try to avoid feelings of envy within ourselves and one of the ways to do this, as mentioned before, is to look at people that are less fortunate than we are. This will soon extinguish any feelings of envy we may harbour towards our brothers and sisters in Islam.

> Do not be envious of one another; do not artificially inflate prices against one another; do not hate one another; do not shun one another; and do not undercut one another in business transactions; and be as fellow-brothers and servants of Allah. A Muslim is the brother of a Muslim. He neither oppresses him nor humiliates him nor looks down upon him. Piety is here – and he pointed to his chest three times. It is evil enough for a Muslim to hold his brother Muslim in contempt. All things of a Muslim are inviolable for another Muslim: his blood, his property and his honour. *(Muslim)*

In Islam, the only time we should compete with each other is in gaining the pleasure of Allah. In one hadith narrated by Abu Huraira, Prophet Muhammad ﷺ said:

There is no desirable form of jealousy except for two types: a person whom Allah has given the Qur'an and he recites it day and night, so when a person hears him he says, 'If only I were given the likes of what he has been given so that I may act upon it the way this person is.' And a person to whom Allah has bestowed wealth and he spends in the cause of Truth, so a person says, 'If only I were given the likes of what he has been given, so that I may act upon it the way this person is.' *(Bukhari)*

General Cures for Diseases of the Heart

As human beings we are prone to making mistakes. In fact, according to some Islamic scholars, the Arabic word for human being *insaan* comes from the Arabic root-word *nasa yansee* which means 'to forget'.

All children of Adam make mistakes and the best among you are the ones who repent (to Allah for their mistakes). *(At-Tirmidhi)*

Every time, we commit a sin, a black spot appears on our heart. If we ask for repentance from Allah and give up the sinful act, then the black spot is removed. If we continue to sin then the black spot grows until the whole heart becomes black (At-Tirmidhi). This is also mentioned in the Qur'an:

Nay! But on their hearts is the Raan (covering of sins and evil deeds) which they used to earn. (Surah Al-Mutaffifin: 14)

Therefore, we must continually seek repentance for our sins and take care that we do not repeat them. Al-Hasan al-Basri, an eminent righteous predecessor, said: "The good deed illuminates the heart and strengthens the body, while the bad deed darkens the heart and weakens the body." In the infinite mercy of Allah, the door of repentance is not closed until the hour of death. However, since none of us know when we shall meet with the Angel of Death, it is best to seek repentance at all times and strive now to purify our hearts as if there is no tomorrow.

The ultimate goal is to attune the heart such that if we commit a wrong action then we feel bad about it within ourselves regardless of what anyone else may say. The first step is to recognise that the human brain has a tremendous ability to rationalise any wrong action to justify committing a sin that appeals to the desires of the *nafs*, thus deceiving the heart. It is easy to confuse the emotions of the ego with the feelings of the heart. Certainly, shaytan uses the rationalising capability of the human brain to silence the truth-seeking voice of the heart. The poet and philosopher, Iqbal, must have been referring to this tremendous capability of the human brain to rationalise when he said in one of his poetic verses:

> "Angel Gabriel (Jibril) told me at the dawn of Life,
> Do not accept the heart that is the slave of the brain.
> Falsehood likes dual nature (hypocrisy) whereas truth is one,
> Do not accept the compromise of truth and falsehood."
> (*Kulliyat Iqbal*)

Maulana Ashraf Ali Thanwi once told his disciples that shaytan had three good qualities (the three A's) but because he lacked the fourth and most important quality, he was expelled from Paradise. Shaytan was a great *Abid* (one who prays a lot), a great *Alim* (scholar of the teachings of all the Prophets of Allah) and a great *Arif* (one who knows the attributes of Allah). However, Satan was not a good *Ashiq* (lover of Allah). For if shaytan had true love of Allah in his heart then he would have submitted to Allah's command to bow to Adam ﷺ without question. [90]

The pure heart cannot love Allah and disobey His commands at the same time. We must live our lives wholly within the teachings of Islam as contained within the Qur'an and Sunnah. The obligatory acts in Islam in themselves provide cures for many diseases. *Salah* is a cure for the disease of heedlessness (*ghafla*), *zakat* is a cure for the love of this world and miserliness (*al-wahn and bukhal*); the fasts of Ramadan are a cure for the diseases of desire (*shahawat*); while Hajj, if performed with sincerity, is the ultimate cure for all diseases of the heart.[91] In addition, the supererogatory acts, such as *nafl salah, sadaqah* and *dhikr*, will cleanse those sins that we have inadvertently committed and prevent us from sinning further. In order to perfect our worship, we should continually seek knowledge and learn about the lawful, unlawful and the doubtful.

> Truly, what is lawful is evident, and what is unlawful is evident, and in between the two are matters which are doubtful which many people do not know. He who guards against doubtful things keeps his religion and honour blameless, and he who indulges in doubtful things indulges in fact in unlawful things,

90. Akhtar, Maulana Hakeem Mohammad (n.d.). *Virtues of Repentance (Tawbah)*. Karachi, Kutab Khana Mazhari.

91. Islahi, Amin Ahsan (2002). *Tazkiyyah Nafs*. Faisalabad, Malik Sons Publishers.

just as a shepherd who pastures his flock round a preserve will soon pasture them in it. Beware, every king has a preserve, and the things Allah has declared unlawful are His preserves. Beware! In the body there is a piece of flesh; if it is sound, the whole body is sound, and if it is corrupt, the whole body is corrupt, and behold, it is the heart. *(Bukhari and Muslim)*

The most perfect worship of Allah comprises a balance of duties towards Allah *(huquq Allah)* and duties towards fellow human beings *(huquq al-ibad)*. They are both equally important and worship is not complete if one is neglected at the expense of the other. *Salah* (which is from *huquq Allah*) is always mentioned together with *zakat* (which is from *huquq al-ibad*) in the Qur'an to emphasise this point.

Spending in the way of Allah encompasses more than merely fulfilling our *zakat* obligations annually. It is when we truly give of the things that we love purely for the sake of Allah that we can achieve *taqwa* (Allah-consciousness).

> *Take provision; but the best provision is the taqwa of Allah. So have taqwa of me, O people of intelligence.* (Surah Al-Baqarah: 197)

It is for this reason that in the Qur'an the word *taqwa* almost always appears with the phrase *infaaq fi sabeel illah* (spending for the sake of Allah).

> *As for him who gives (in charity) and keeps his duty to Allah and fears Him, And believes in Al-Husna. We will make smooth for him the path of ease (goodness). But he who is greedy miser and thinks himself*

self-sufficient. And gives the lie to Al-Husna. We will make smooth for him the path for evil. (Surah Al-Lail: 5-10)

The few simple words of the following hadith, narrated by Abu Huraira, give us the basis on which to conduct our lives so that we can, insha'Allah, achieve *Qalb Saleem.*

The Prophet 鬘 said, "I testify to three things; that giving sadaqah does not decrease your capital; when the slave forgives his brother for the sake of Allah, Allah gives him honour and whoever humbles himself before Allah, Allah will raise his degree." *(Muslim)*

CHAPTER FIVE

Concluding Remarks

HUMAN BEINGS ARE comprised of body and soul. The body represents the terrestrial aspect of humans whereas the soul is the celestial aspect. The point where the two meet is the human heart. In other words, the heart acts as a window between the earthly and the heavenly. In Islam, the heart has always been regarded as an organ of intelligence, capable of understanding. In order to achieve salvation in the Hereafter, the heart must be purified from spiritual blemishes. According to the Islamic approach, the mind and heart, body and soul all work in unison, not independently of each other.

Western thinkers and philosophers throughout the years have viewed the human body as a machine that carries out biological and chemical processes and stripped it of any spiritual values. Thus the heart and brain have been separated, with the role of the heart reduced to that of a pumping machine. This separation was a consequence of the separation of religious and secular matters in Western education and society.

Nevertheless, a branch of modern science is emerging that acknowledges what the Qur'an has been stating for the last 1400 years – that the human heart is an organ capable of emotion, understanding and communication. In fact, there is constant communication between the brain and heart and the heart exerts some influence over the brain. However, science has its limitations as Carl Jung, the famous psychologist, once said:

> "Science can denature plutonium but it cannot denature evil in the heart of man."

To denature evil in the heart of man can only and successfully be done by religion. In Islam, the heart can be regarded as an organ both of conscience and consciousness. On the other hand, the brain is an organ of consciousness alone. Hence, the heart has a more important role to play than the brain in the spiritual realm because of the heart's importance in creating a value system based on justice and fair play. These are the foundations for every individual and every healthy society.

It is important to stress at this stage that the Qur'an does not deny the existence and importance of the human brain. The brain is in fact the biggest data storage system in our body. All the materialistic scientific progress that we are seeing today is due to the miraculous powers of the brain. But since that progress is made with the denial of the intellect of the heart, it is devoid of any spiritual or ethical values. The human brain with its rational and material reasoning is incapable of understanding spirituality and our relationship to God; it is like trying to weigh a whole mountain with the help of a goldsmith's pair of scales, as noted by

Ibn Khaldun in his famous *Muqaddimah* of History.

This book has emphasised the importance of the science of *tazkiyyah*, the purification of the heart, in this age of materialism where the emphasis is on the brain. In order to be complete as human beings, we must recognise and accept the importance of the heart's wisdom together with the intellect of the brain. According to a hadith of Prophet Muhammad ﷺ, the Dajjal (anti-Christ) is said to have only one eye (Ibn Majah). When we trivialise the role and function of the heart in our lives, then we end up with a very limited view of the world as if we have only one eye. However, when our heart and brain waves act in synchrony, our thoughts become more focused and rational. We need to have our hearts and brains in order because that is the balance of *batin* (inward) and *zahir* (outward). Finally, we need to always remember the words of the Prophet Muhammad ﷺ:

> Indeed there is in the body a piece of flesh which if it is sound then the whole body is sound, and if it is corrupt then the whole body is corrupt. Indeed it is the heart. *(Bukhari and Muslim)*

Appendix I:
The First Heart Surgery

AN IMPORTANT INCIDENT happened in the life of Prophet Muhammad ﷺ when he reached the age of about five. At that time, he was living with his wet nurse, Halimah, a Bedouin woman from the tribe of Banu Sa'd, in her village. That incident scared Halimah so much that she decided to take the child (Prophet Muhammad ﷺ) back to his mother, Aminah, in Makkah. The details of the incident as Safi-ur-Rehman Mubarakpoori has described it in his book 'The Sealed Nectar' (a biography of Prophet Muhammad ﷺ) are as follows:

> "Then, as related by Anas in *Sahih Muslim*, Jibril came down and ripped his chest open and took out the heart. He then extracted a blood clot out of it and said: "That was the part of Satan in thee." And then he washed it with the water of Zamzam in a gold basin. After that the heart was joined together and restored to its place. The boys and playmates came running to his mother, i.e. his wet-nurse, and said: "Verily, Muhammad ﷺ has been murdered." They all rushed towards him and found him alright, only his face was white."[92]

---

92. Mubarakpuri, Safi ur Rehman (1996). *The Sealed Nectar* (in Urdu). Lahore, Al-Maktabatul Salafiyya.

Ibn Sa'd in his *Kitab al-Tabaqat al-Kabir* has also added that the water used by angels to wash the heart of Prophet Muhammad ﷺ was ice-cold.[93] At the time that this miracle was performed, it was beyond human imagination that the chest could be cut open and the human heart taken out and replaced. Yet, today open-heart surgery is a normal procedure. That also tells us about the knowledge of the Prophet ﷺ who could foretell of events in the distant future.

Sheikh Hamza Yusuf has drawn some very interesting parallels between the miraculous first heart surgery of the Prophet and modern-day heart surgery. Angels, who performed the miraculous heart surgery, are made of light and today heart surgery is performed with the use of laser light. When the veins and arteries connecting the heart to the body are cut, the heart continues to beat for a while, but will eventually die. In order to keep it alive, it is necessary to slow down its metabolism and in modern surgery this is done by placing it in ice-cold saline (salty) water. Historically, Zamzam water had more salt content 1400 years ago as compared to today. The angels took out the heart of Prophet Muhammad ﷺ after ripping his chest open and washed it with the ice-cold saline water of Zamzam and then the heart was joined together and restored to its place. [94]

In fact, in a hadith narrated by Hakim (a book of the traditions of Prophet Muhammad ﷺ), Anas bin Malik ﷺ also reported seeing the imprints of sutures in the middle of the chest of Prophet Muhammad ﷺ. This tradition has been regarded as authentic

---

93. Ibn Sa'd, Abu Abdullah Muhammad (n.d.). *Kitab Al-Tabaqat Al-Kabir*. New Delhi, Kitab Bhavan.
94. Yusuf, Hamza *Al-Isra' wal Mi'raj* (video speech; 2001). Hayward, Alhambra Productions.

(sahih) by Hakim as mentioned by as-Suyuti in his book *Al-Khasais al-Kubra*.[95] The imprints of sutures on the chest of Prophet Muhammad ﷺ were caused by the heart surgery performed by the angels of Allah.

The purpose of this miracle was to purify the Prophet's ﷺ heart and to prepare it to receive direct revelation from Allah in the form of the Qur'an:

> *And truly, this (the Qur'an) is a revelation from the Lord of the 'Alamin (all living creatures in the Universe), which the trustworthy 'Ruh' (Jibril) has brought down upon your heart (O Muhammad) that you may be (one) of the warners.* (Surah Ash-Shu'ara: 192-194)

Allah chose the heart of the Prophet Muhammad ﷺ for the direct revelation of the Qur'an on it. No other human beings' heart had the strength to receive direct revelation. The miracle of the purification of his heart was also performed to enable the Prophet's ﷺ heart to see the Greatest Signs of his Lord during the night journey *(Al-Isra wal-Mi'raj)* to the heavens as described in the Qur'an:

> *The (Prophet's) heart lied not (in seeing) what he saw. Will you then dispute with him (Muhammad ﷺ) about what he saw (during the Mi'raj)?* (Surah An-Najm: 11-12)

---

95. Suyyuti, Imam Jalaluddin (2003). *Al-Khasais al-Kubra*. Lahore, Maktaba A'la Hadhrat.

Appendix II: History of the Science of Tazkiyyah

A study of the early history of Islam reveals that the rules of the sciences of *tafseer* (Qur'anic commentary), *hadith* (traditions of Prophet Muhammad ﷺ) and *fiqh* (Islamic jurisprudence) were not compiled during the time of the Companions of Prophet Muhammad ﷺ but they nonetheless existed during the time of the Prophet and his Companions. Similarly, the science of *tazkiyyah* (the purification of the heart) also existed from the very inception of Islam. The rules of all these sciences were complied during the time of the *tabi'een* (pious successors to the Companions).

Ibn Khaldun, the fourteenth century Islamic historian, in the *Muqaddimah* (Prolegomena of History) pointed out that in the first three generations of Islam, the science of Islamic spirituality was too general to have a specific name. However, when worldliness became prevalent and people started to become more and more occupied with the activities of the material pursuits of life, a group of people dedicated themselves to the worship of God and they distinguished themselves from the materialist people.[96]

---

96. Ibn Khaldun, Abdur Rahman (1993). *Muqadimmah Tarekh Ibn Khaldun*. Lahore, Al-Faisal Publishers and Traders.

All great scholars during the early stages of Islam were aware of *tazkiyyah* and many wrote books on this subject. These include:

- ❀ Imam Abdullah bin Mubarak (118 - 181 A.H.), *Kitab az-Zuhd* (Book of Piety)
- ❀ Imam Ahmad bin Hanbal (164 - 241 A.H.), *Kitab az-Zuhd* (Book of Piety)
- ❀ Imam Harith bin Asad al-Muhasibi (165 - 243 A.H.), *Kitab az-Zuhd* (Book of Piety)
- ❀ Imam Abu Hamid al-Ghazali (450 - 505 A.H.), *Ihya Ulum ad-Din* (Revival of the Religious Sciences), regarded as the definitive book on the subject of *tazkiyyah*
- ❀ Imam Ibn Taymiyyah, *Amradhul Quloob wa Shifa'uha* (Diseases of the Hearts and Their Cures) (661 - 728 A.H.), a treatise that can be found in his multi-voluminous *Fatawa Imam Ibn Taymiyyah.*
- ❀ Allama Ibn al-Qayyim al-Jawziya, the great student of Imam Ibn Taymiyyah (691 - 751 A.H.), *Madarij us-Salikeen* (Stations of the seekers of purification)
- ❀ Abdur Rahman Ibn Jawzee (511 - 597 A.H.), *Minhaj ul Qasideen* (Middle Path for the Seekers of Guidance)
- ❀ Maulana Jalaluddin Rumi (604 - 672 A.H.), *Mathnawi*
- ❀ Shah Wali Ullah Dehlawi, *Hujjatullah Al-Balighah* (Perfect Proof of Allah)
- ❀ Sheikh Abdul Qadir Jilani (470 - 561 A.H.), *Ghaniyatu Talibeen* (Wealth of the Seekers of Purification)
- ❀ Imam Abul Qasim Al-Qushayri (376 - 465 A.H.), *Risala Qushayria* (A Treatise by Qushayri)
- ❀ Abu Talib Makki (died 386 A.H.), *Qoowatul Quloob* (Strength of the Hearts)

These scholars were well versed in the science of *tazkiyyah* and at the same time they were great scholars of the traditions of Prophet Muhammad ﷺ *(muhaditheen)*. They presented the principles of Islam clearly, making Islamic spirituality accessible to everyone so that people could learn and thus purify their hearts. We can still benefit from the books written by our great scholars *(ulama salaf)*. These people were in reality the Islamic psychologists who excelled in the science of Islamic Spirituality and Islamic Psychology. But most importantly, they were strict adherents to the Sunnah of the Prophet ﷺ. As Sheikh Junaid Baghdadi (who is considered to be one of the greatest experts of the science of *tazkiyyah*) said:

> "If a person appears to be a great saint of Allah and he is walking on water and saying prayers on a 'sajjadah' in the air but if he is performing a single act against the sunnah of Prophet Muhammad ﷺ then this person is not a saint of Allah; rather he is a devil *(inahu laisa bi wali in inahu shaitan)*."

BLESSING OR CURSE

Everything or everyone could be a blessing or curse depending on what they pull you toward.

* HUSBANDS
* CHILDREN
* WEALTH
* FRIENDS
* JOB
* HOBBIES
* WIFES etc etc

Everything and everyone should be a blessing in pulling you towards

PARADISE